DATE DUE		
OCP 2 6 / NOV 1 4 / MAY 0		
DEC 8 2000		
OCT1 8 '99		
NOV 02 99		
NOV 02 99		
JAN 17 00		
FEB 23 00		
MAR 29 00		
APR 10 00		

Shakespeare

Complete poems

WILLIAM SHAKESPEARE

Complete
Poems

WILLIAM SHAKESPEARE

Complete Poems

j822.3
Jha

GRAMERCY BOOKS
New York • Avenel,

Introduction and compilation
Copyright © 1993 by Outlet Book Company, Inc.
All rights reserved

This edition is published by Gramercy Books,
distributed by Outlet Book Company, Inc.,
a Random House Company,
40 Engelhard Avenue,
Avenel, New Jersey 07001.

Random House
New York · Toronto · London · Sydney · Auckland

Printed and bound in the United States

Library of Congress Cataloging-in-Publication Data
Shakespeare, William, 1564–1616.
[Poems]
Complete poems of William Shakespeare.
p.   cm.
ISBN: 0-517-09382-0
I. Title.
PR2841   1993   93-7891
822.3′3—dc20   CIP

8 7 6 5 4 3 2

CONTENTS

INTRODUCTION

In his lifetime, William Shakespeare personally super-
vised the publication of only two works, the narrative
poems *Venus and Adonis* and *The Rape of Lucrece*. (The
First Folio, a collection of his plays was not published
until 1623, seven years after his death.) Although he was
one of the greatest poets in the English language, he was,
above all, a practical man of the theater. He was a pros-
perous playwright, actor, and partner in a thriving theat-
rical company. He had an almost infallible commercial
instinct. His plays were both popular and critical suc-
cesses and he became wealthy by tailoring his art to the
tastes of the Elizabethan public. Although most plays in
Shakespeare's day were written in verse, they were
meant to be performed and not read, since publication
would have given rival theater companies access to them.
At that time, plays were properties and closely guarded
by the theater companies that owned and produced
them. Nondramatic poetry, like the works of Shakespeare collected in this volume, was intended for publication since it was considered a legitimate literary effort.

Venus and Adonis and *The Rape of Lucrece* were
written and published between 1592 and 1594 when the
London theaters were closed because of the plague. The
sudden cessation and questionable future of his livelihood probably prodded Shakespeare into considering a
literary career outside the theater. Both were dedicated
to Henry Wriothesley, the Earl of Southampton, a young
nobleman who at the time was becoming known as a
patron of poets. Both are erotic narrative poems based on
the style of the great Latin poet Ovid, a genre that was

extremely popular at the end of the sixteenth century. *Venus and Adonis* was widely imitated and there are more contemporary allusions to it than any other of Shakespeare's works. It went through ten editions during his lifetime and was his most reprinted work. Based on the tenth book of Ovid's *Metamorphoses*, it is a retelling of the mythical tale of the wooing of Adonis, the beautiful mortal, by Venus, the Roman goddess of love. In a major change from the original, Shakespeare transforms Adonis from a willing lover into a reluctant and bashful boy, which yields some engagingly humorous situations.

The Rape of Lucrece was also popular and went through six editions in Shakespeare's lifetime. It is apparently the "graver labor" he promised in the dedication to Southampton in the earlier work. It is based on Ovid's *Fasti* and Livy's history of Rome, and recounts the violation of Lucrece, a Roman noblewoman, by Tarquin, a member of Rome's ruling family. It was an event which precipitated a rebellion against Rome's dictators and the formation of the Roman republic, but Shakespeare chose to focus on the private side of the story, highlighting the dramatic passions of the victim and the rapist. The work was important because it laid the foundation for Shakespeare's later Roman history plays and explored important themes which were to recur in his subsequent tragedies. Tarquin is clearly a study in self-destructive evil which he later perfected in his portrait of Macbeth.

The *Sonnets* were published in 1609, apparently without Shakespeare's permission since the dedication was not written by Shakespeare but by Thomas Thorpe, the publisher. Francis Meres in his *Palladis Tamia* of 1598 speaks of Shakespeare's "sugared sonnets among his private friends," and most scholars believe they were written between 1592 and 1596 and, perhaps, revised and rearranged at a later date. They, too, reveal how attuned Shakespeare was to public tastes. A fad for sonnet cycles in England had begun in 1591, with the publication of Sir Philip Sidney's *Astrophel and Stella*, and lasted until the end of the century. In keeping with the conventions of the genre, Shakespeare also wrote *A Lover's Complaint* (published in the volume with the *Sonnets*) following the example of Samuel Daniel who added a poem called *The Complaint of Rosamond* to *Delia*, his popular 1592 sonnet cycle. (Complaint poems about women, usually historical figures, were also in vogue at the time.) But that is where the comparison ends, for Shakespeare's is the greatest surviving sonnet cycle of the Elizabethan era and it surpasses the others in psychological depth and complexity as well as ingenuity.

Shakespeare's sonnets deviate significantly from other cycles. Most of the poems, the first one hundred and twenty-six, are addressed to the poet's patron, a beautiful young nobleman, and are concerned with their friendship. Usually in such sonnet cycles, the person addressed was an idealized and virtuous young woman who the poet was courting. Although sonnets 127 to 152 relate to the poet's mistress, they invoke an image of an irresistibly sensual "Dark Lady." She is a woman of questionable morals for it is implied that she has also seduced the poet's young friend. The inherent drama of this romantic triangle and the writer's unmistakable anguish have fascinated generations of readers with speculations about the biographical link to Shakespeare's own life. The favored candidate for the young man is Henry Wriothesley, to whom Shakespeare dedicated his two earlier narrative poems—although his initials reverse the order of Thorpe's dedicatee. As for the "Dark Lady," there has been little evidence for a confident guess.

The great English Romantic poet William Wordsworth said of the *Sonnets*, "With this key Shakespeare unlocked his heart." The poet Robert Browning retorted, "Did Shakespeare? If so the less Shakespeare he!" In reality they are probably a blend of fact and fiction. It is a mystery that will never be resolved and provides an endless and enjoyable puzzle. But this in no way obscures the literary merit of the sonnets themselves, for the best are among the greatest love poems ever written.

That Shakespeare was a bankable name is demonstrated by the case of *The Passionate Pilgrim*, published in 1599. It is a miscellaneous collection of poems attributed to Shakespeare by its unscrupulous publisher, William Jaggard. The volume did contain poems by Shakespeare, two sonnets (138 and 144) and three songs (3, 5, and 16) from his play *Love's Labor's Lost*. But it also included works by other poets, including a version of Christopher Marlowe's "The Passionate Shepherd to His Love." There are eleven poems (included here in this book) whose authorship cannot be determined, but are traditionally credited to Shakespeare.

The Phoenix and Turtle was published in 1601 as part of Robert Chester's *Love's Martyr: or Rosalind's Complaint*, which also included poems by Ben Jonson and George Chapman. The turtle in the title is a turtledove, symbolic for constancy in love; the phoenix is the immortal mythical bird which is reborn from its own ashes after its death on a funeral pyre. Most scholars believe that for Elizabethans the poem had an allegorical meaning that has now been lost. It is a strange and unique poem, unlike anything else that Shakespeare wrote.

Ben Jonson, Shakespeare's friend and a rival playwright, called him the "star of poets." It is impossible to disagree after reading the poems collected in this volume. His verse continues to touch our hearts and counsel our souls. Today, readers reach the same conclusion that Jonson did almost four hundred years ago, "He was not of an age, but for all time."

CHRISTOPHER MORE

New York
1993

Venus
and Adonis

TO THE RIGHT HONORABLE HENRY WRIOTHESLY,
EARL OF SOUTHAMPTON, AND BARON OF TICHFIELD

RIGHT HONORABLE, I know not how I shall offend in dedicating my unpolished lines to your lordship, nor how the world will censure me for choosing so strong a prop to support so weak a burden: only, if your honor seem but pleased, I account myself highly praised, and vow to take advantage of all idle hours, till I have honored you with some graver labor. But if the first heir of my invention prove deformed, I shall be sorry it had so noble a godfather, and never after ear so barren a land, for fear it yield me still so bad a harvest. I leave it to your honorable survey, and your honor to your heart's content; which I wish may always answer your own wish, and the world's hopeful expectation.

Your honor's in all duty,
William Shakespeare

VENUS AND ADONIS

Even as the sun with purple-colored face
Had ta'en his last leave of the weeping morn,
Rose-cheeked Adonis hied him to the chase;
Hunting he loved, but love he laughed to scorn.
  Sick-thoughted Venus makes amain unto him,
  And like a bold-faced suitor 'gins to woo him.

"Thrice fairer than myself," thus she began,
"The field's chief flower, sweet above compare,
Stain to all nymphs, more lovely than a man,
More white and red than doves or roses are:
  Nature that made thee, with herself at strife,
  Saith that the world hath ending with thy life.

"Vouchsafe, thou wonder, to alight thy steed,
And rein his proud head to the saddlebow;
If thou wilt deign this favor, for thy meed
A thousand honey secrets shalt thou know:
  Here come and sit, where never serpent hisses,
  And being set, I'll smother thee with kisses;

"And yet not cloy thy lips with loathed satiety,
But rather famish them amid their plenty,
Making them red and pale with fresh variety—
Ten kisses short as one, one long as twenty:
  A summer's day will seem an hour but short,
  Being wasted in such time-beguiling sport."

With this she seizeth on his sweating palm,
The precedent of pith and livelihood,
And, trembling in her passion, calls it balm,

Earth's sovereign salve to do a goddess good:
  Being so enraged, desire doth lend her force
  Courageously to pluck him from his horse.

Over one arm the lusty courser's rein,
Under her other was the tender boy,
Who blushed and pouted in a dull disdain,
With leaden appetite, unapt to toy;
  She red and hot as coals of glowing fire,
  He red for shame, but frosty in desire.

The studded bridle on a ragged bough
Nimbly she fastens; (O, how quick is love!)
The steed is stallèd up, and even now
To tie the rider she begins to prove:
  Backward she pushed him, as she would be thrust,
  And governed him in strength, though not in lust.

So soon was she along, as he was down,
Each leaning on their elbows and their hips:
Now doth she stroke his cheek, now doth he frown,
And 'gins to chide, but soon she stops his lips;
  And kissing, speaks, with lustful language broken,
  "If thou wilt chide, thy lips shall never open."

He burns with bashful shame; she with her tears
Doth quench the maiden burning of his cheeks:
Then with her windy sighs and golden hairs,
To fan and blow them dry again she seeks:
  He saith she is immodest, blames her miss,
  What follows more she murders with a kiss.

Even as an empty eagle, sharp by fast,
Tires with her beak on feathers, flesh, and bone,
Shaking her wings, devouring all in haste,

Till either gorge be stuffed, or prey be gone;
    Even so she kissed his brow, his cheek, his chin,
    And where she ends she doth anew begin.

Forced to content, but never to obey,
Panting he lies, and breatheth in her face;
She feedeth on the steam as on a prey,
And calls it heavenly moisture, air of grace;
    Wishing her cheeks were gardons full of flowers,
    So they were dewed with such distilling showers.

Look, how a bird lies tangled in a net,
So fastened in her arms Adonis lies;
Pure shame and awed resistance made him fret,
Which bred more beauty in his angry eyes:
    Rain added to a river that is rank,
    Perforce will force it overflow the bank.

Still she entreats, and prettily entreats,
For to a pretty ear she tunes her tale;
Still is he sullen, still he lours and frets,
'Twixt crimson shame and anger ashy-pale;
    Being red, she loves him best; and being white,
    Her best is bettered with a more delight.

Look how he can, she cannot choose but love;
And by her fair immortal hand she swears
From his soft bosom never to remove,
Till he take truce with her contending tears,
    Which long have rained, making her cheeks all wet;
    And one sweet kiss shall pay this countless debt.

Upon this promise did he raise his chin,
Like a dive dapper peering through a wave,
Who, being looked on, ducks as quickly in;

So offers he to give what she did crave;
  But when her lips were ready for his pay,
  He winks, and turns his lips another way.

Never did passenger in summer's heat
More thirst for drink than she for this good turn:
Her help she sees, but help she cannot get;
She bathes in water, yet her fire must burn:
  "O, pity," 'gan she cry, "flint-hearted boy!
  'Tis but a kiss I beg; why art thou coy?

"I have been wooed, as I entreat thee now,
Even by the stern and direful god of war,
Whose sinewy neck in battle ne'er did bow,
Who conquers where he comes, in every jar;
  Yet hath he been my captive and my slave,
  And begged for that which thou unasked shalt have.

"Over my altars hath he hung his lance,
His battered shield, his uncontrollèd crest,
And for my sake hath learned to sport and dance,
To toy, to wanton, dally, smile, and jest;
  Scorning his churlish drum, and ensign red,
  Making my arms his field, his tent my bed.

"Thus he that overruled I overswayed,
Leading him prisoner in a red-rose chain:
Strong-tempered steel his stronger strength obeyed,
Yet was he servile to my coy disdain.
  O, be not proud, nor brag not of thy might,
  For mast'ring her that foiled the god of fight!

"Touch but my lips with those fair lips of thine—
Though mine be not so fair, yet are they red—
The kiss shall be thine own as well as mine—
What see'st thou in the ground? Hold up thy head;

Look in mine eyeballs, there thy beauty lies;
Then why not lips on lips, since eyes in eyes?

"Art thou ashamed to kiss? Then wink again,
And I will wink; so shall the day seem night;
Love keeps his revels where there are but twain;
Be bold to play, our sport is not in sight:
    These blue-veined violets whereupon we lean
    Never can blab, nor know not what we mean.

"The tender spring upon thy tempting lip
Shows thee unripe: yet mayst thou well be tasted:
Make use of time, let not advantage slip;
Beauty within itself should not be wasted:
    Fair flowers that are not gathered in their prime
    Rot and consume themselves in little time.

"Were I hard-favored, foul, or wrinkled-old,
Ill-natured, crooked, churlish, harsh in voice,
O'erworn, despisèd, rheumatic, and cold,
Thick-sighted, barren, lean, and lacking juice,
    Then mightst thou pause, for then I were not for
        thee;
    But having no defects, why dost abhor me?

"Thou canst not see one wrinkle in my brow;
Mine eyes are gray, and bright, and quick in turning;
My beauty as the spring doth yearly grow,
My flesh is soft and plump, my marrow burning;
    My smooth moist hand, were it with thy hand felt,
    Would in thy palm dissolve, or seem to melt.

"Bid me discourse, I will enchant thine ear,
Or, like a fairy, trip upon the green,
Or, like a nymph, with long disheveled hair,
Dance on the sands, and yet no footing seen:

Love is a spirit all compact of fire,
Not gross to sink, but light, and will aspire.

"Witness this primrose bank whereon I lie;
These forceless flowers like sturdy trees support me;
Two strengthless doves will draw me through the sky,
From morn till night, even where I list to sport me:
    Is love so light, sweet boy, and may it be
    That thou shouldst think it heavy unto thee?

"Is thine own heart to thine own face affected?
Can thy right hand seize love upon thy left?
Then woo thyself, be of thyself rejected,
Steal thine own freedom, and complain on theft.
    Narcissus so himself himself forsook,
    And died to kiss his shadow in the brook.

"Torches are made to light, jewels to wear,
Dainties to taste, fresh beauty for the use,
Herbs for their smell, and sappy plants to bear;
Things growing to themselves are growth's abuse:
    Seeds spring from seeds, and beauty breedeth
        beauty,
    Thou wast begot—to get it is thy duty.

"Upon the earth's increase why shouldst thou feed,
Unless the earth with thy increase be fed?
By law of nature thou art bound to breed,
That thine may live, when thou thyself art dead;
    And so, in spite of death, thou dost survive,
    In that thy likeness still is left alive."

By this, the lovesick queen began to sweat,
For, where they lay, the shadow had forsook them,
And Titan, tired in the midday heat,

With burning eye did hotly overlook them;
  Wishing Adonis had his team to guide,
  So he were like him, and by Venus' side.

And now Adonis, with a lazy sprite,
And with a heavy, dark, disliking eye,
His louring brows o'erwhelming his fair sight,
Like misty vapors when they blot the sky—
  Souring his cheeks, cries, "Fie, no more of love!
  The sun doth burn my face; I must remove."

"Ah me," quoth Venus, "young, and so unkind?
What bare excuses mak'st thou to be gone!
I'll sigh celestial breath, whose gentle wind
Shall cool the heat of this descending sun:
  I'll make a shadow for thee of my hairs;
  If they burn too, I'll quench them with my tears.

"The sun that shines from heaven shines but warm,
And, lo, I lie between that sun and thee!
The heat I have from thence doth little harm,
Thine eye darts forth the fire that burneth me;
  And were I not immortal, life were done,
  Between this heavenly and earthly sun.

"Art thou obdurate, flinty, hard as steel,
Nay, more than flint, for stone at rain relenteth?
Art thou a woman's son, and canst not feel
What 'tis to love? How want of love tormenteth?
  O, had thy mother borne so hard a mind,
  She had not brought forth thee, but died unkind!

"What am I, that thou shouldst contemn me this?
Or what great danger swells upon my suit?
What were thy lips the worse for one poor kiss?

Speak, fair; but speak fair words, or else be mute:
Give me one kiss, I'll give it thee again,
And one for int'rest, if thou wilt have twain.

"Fie, lifeless picture, cold and senseless stone,
Well-painted idol, image dull and dead,
Statue, contenting but the eye alone,
Thing like a man, but of no woman bred!
Thou art no man, though of a man's complexion,
For men will kiss even by their own direction."

This said, impatience chokes her pleading tongue,
And swelling passion doth provoke a pause;
Red cheeks and fiery eyes blaze forth her wrong,
Being judge in love, she cannot right her cause:
And now she weeps, and now she fain would speak,
And now her sobs do her intendments break.

Sometimes she shakes her head, and then his hand,
Now gazeth she on him, now on the ground;
Sometimes her arms infold him like a band:
She would, he will not in her arms be bound;
And when from thence he struggles to be gone,
She locks her lily fingers one in one.

"Fondling," she said, "since I have hemmed thee here,
Within the circuit of this ivory pale,
I'll be a park, and thou shalt be my deer;
Feed where thou wilt, on mountain or in dale:
Graze on my lips; and if those hills be dry,
Stray lower, where the pleasant fountains lie.

"Within this limit is relief enough,
Sweet bottom grass, and high delightful plain,
Round rising hillocks, brakes obscure and rough,

To shelter thee from tempest and from rain:
  Then be my deer, since I am such a park;
  No dog shall rouse thee, though a thousand bark."

At this Adonis smiles as in disdain,
That in each cheek appears a pretty dimple:
Love made those hollows, if himself were slain,
He might be buried in a tomb so simple;
  Foreknowing well, if there he came to lie,
  Why, there Love lived, and there he could not die.

These lovely caves, these round enchanting pits,
Opened their mouths to swallow Venus' liking:
Being mad before, how doth she now for wits?
Struck dead at first, what needs a second striking?
  Poor queen of love, in thine own law forlorn,
  To love a cheek that smiles at thee in scorn!

Now which way shall she turn? What shall she say?
Her words are done, her woes the more increasing;
The time is spent, her object will away,
And from her twining arms doth urge releasing:
  "Pity," she cries, "some favor—some remorse!"
  Away he springs, and hasteth to his horse.

But, lo, from forth a copse that neighbors by,
A breeding jennet, lusty, young, and proud,
Adonis' trampling courser doth espy,
And forth she rushes, snorts, and neighs aloud:
  The strong-necked steed, being tied unto a tree,
  Breaketh his rein, and to her straight goes he.

Imperiously he leaps, he neighs, he bounds,
And now his woven girths he breaks asunder;
The bearing earth with his hard hoof he wounds,

Whose hollow womb resounds like heaven's thunder:
The iron bit he crushes 'tween his teeth,
Controlling what he was controllèd with.

His ears uppricked; his braided hanging mane
Upon his compassed crest now stand on end;
His nostrils drink the air, and forth again,
As from a furnace, vapors doth he send:
  His eye, which scornfully glisters like fire,
  Shows his hot courage and his high desire.

Sometime he trots, as if he told the steps,
With gentle majesty and modest pride;
Anon he rears upright, curvets and leaps,
As who should say, "Lo, thus my strength is tried,
  And this I do to captivate the eye
  Of the fair breeder that is standing by."

What recketh he his rider's angry stir,
His flattering "Holla," or his "Stand, I say?"
What cares he now for curb or pricking spur?
For rich caparisons or trapping gay?
  He sees his love, and nothing else he sees,
  Nor nothing else with his proud sight agrees.

Look, when a painter would surpass the life,
In limning out a well-proportioned steed,
His art with nature's workmanship at strife,
As if the dead the living should exceed;
  So did this horse excel a common one,
  In shape, in courage, color, pace, and bone.

Round-hoofed, short-jointed, fetlocks shag and long,
Broad breast, full eye, small head, and nostril wide,
High crest, short ears, straight legs, and passing strong

Thick mane, thick tail, broad buttock, tender hid
Look, what a horse should have he did not lacl
Save a proud rider on so proud a back.

Sometimes he scuds far off, and there he stares;
Anon he starts at stirring of a feather;
To bid the wind a base he now prepares,
And whe'er he run or fly they know not whether;
　For through his mane and tail the high wind sings,
　Fanning the hairs, who wave like feathered wings.

He looks upon his love, and neighs unto her;
She answers him, as if she knew his mind:
Being proud, as females are, to see him woo her,
She puts on outward strangeness, seems unkind;
　Spurns at his love, and scorns the heat he feels,
　Beating his kind embracements with her heels.

Then, like a melancholy malcontent,
He vails his tail, that, like a falling plume,
Cool shadow to his melting buttock lent:
He stamps, and bites the poor flies in his fume.
　His love, perceiving how he is enraged,
　Grew kinder, and his fury was assuaged.

His testy master goeth about to take him;
When, lo, the unbacked breeder, full of fear,
Jealous of catching, swiftly doth forsake him,
With her horse, and left Adonis there:
　As they were mad, unto the wood they hie them,
　Outstripping crows that strive to overfly them.

All swollen with chafing down Adonis sits,
Banning his boisterous and unruly beast:
And now the happy season once more fits,

That lovesick love by pleading may be blest;
  For lovers say, the heart hath treble wrong
  When it is barred the aidance of the tongue.

An oven that is stopped, or river stayed,
Burneth more hotly, swelleth more with rage:
So of concealèd sorrow may be said;
Free vent of words love's fire doth assuage;
  But when the heart's attorney once is mute,
  The client breaks, as desperate in his suit.

He sees her coming, and begins to glow,
Even as a dying coal revives with wind,
And with his bonnet hides his angry brow;
Looks on the dull earth with disturbèd mind;
  Taking no notice that she is so nigh,
  For all askance he holds her in his eye.

O, what a sight it was, wistly to view
How she came stealing to the wayward boy!
To note the fighting conflict of her hue,
How white and red each other did destroy!
  But now her cheek was pale, and by and by
  It flashed forth fire, as lightning from the sky.

Now was she just before him as he sat,
And like a lowly lover down she kneels;
With one fair hand she heaveth up his hat,
Her other tender hand his fair cheek feels:
  His tend'rer cheek receives her soft hand's print,
  As apt as new-fallen snow takes any dint.

O, what a war of looks was there between them!
Her eyes, petitioners, to his eyes suing;
His eyes saw her eyes as they had not seen them;

Her eyes wooed still, his eyes disdained the wooing:
  And all this dumb play had his acts made plain
  With tears, which, chorus-like, her eyes did rain.

Full gently now she takes him by the hand,
A lily prisoned in a jail of snow,
Or ivory in an alabaster band;
So white a friend engirts so white a foe:
  This beauteous combat, willful and unwilling,
  Showed like two silver doves that sit a-billing.

Once more the engine of her thoughts began:
"O, fairest mover on this mortal round,
Would thou wert as I am, and I a man,
My heart as whole as thine, thy heart my wound;
  For one sweet look thy help I would assure thee,
  Though nothing but my body's bane would cure thee."

"Give me my hand," said he. "Why dost thou feel it?"
"Give me my heart," said she, "and thou shalt have it;
O, give it me, lest thy hard heart do steel it,
And being steeled, soft sighs can never grave it:
  Then love's deep groans I never shall regard,
  Because Adonis' heart hath made mine hard."

"For shame," he cries, "let go, and let me go;
My day's delight is past, my horse is gone,
And 'tis your fault I am bereft him so;
I pray you hence, and leave me here alone;
  For all my mind, my thought, my busy care,
  Is how to get my palfrey from the mare."

Thus she replies: "Thy palfrey, as he should,
Welcomes the warm approach of sweet desire:
Affection is a coal that must be cooled;

Else, suffered, it will set the heart on fire:
The sea hath bounds, but deep desire hath none;
Therefore no marvel though thy horse be gone.

"How like a jade he stood, tied to the tree,
Servilely mastered with a leathern rein!
But when he saw his love, his youth's fair fee,
He held such petty bondage in disdain;
Throwing the base thong from his bending crest,
Enfranchising his mouth, his back, his breast.

"Who sees his truelove in her naked bed
Teaching the sheets a whiter hue than white,
But, when his glutton eye so full hath fed,
His other agents aim at like delight?
Who is so faint that dare not be bold
To touch the fire, the weather being cold?

"Let me excuse thy courser, gentle boy;
And learn of him, I heartily beseech thee,
To take advantage on presented joy;
Though I were dumb, yet his proceedings teach thee:
O, learn to love! The lesson is but plain,
And once made perfect, never lost again."

"I know not love," quoth he, "nor will not know it,
Unless it be a boar, and then I chase it;
'Tis much to borrow, and I will not owe it;
My love to love is love but to disgrace it;
For I have heard it is a life in death,
That laughs, that weeps, and all but with a breath.

"Who wears a garment shapeless and unfinished?
Who plucks the bud before one leaf put forth?
If springing things be any jot diminished,
They wither in their prime, prove nothing worth:

The colt that's backed and burdened being young,
Loseth his pride, and never waxeth strong.

"You hurt my hand with wringing; let us part,
And leave this idle theme, this bootless chat:
Remove your siege from my unyielding heart;
To love's alarms it will not ope the gate:
    Dismiss your vows, your feignèd tears, your
        flatt'ry;
    For where a heart is hard, they make no batt'ry."

"What, canst thou talk?" quoth she. "Hast thou a tongue?
O, would thou hadst not, or I had no hearing!
Thy mermaid's voice hath done me double wrong;
I had my load before, now pressed with bearing:
    Melodious discord, heavenly tune harsh sounding,
    Earth's deep-sweet music, and heart's deep-sore
        wounding.

"Had I no eyes but ears, my ears would love
That inward beauty and invisible;
Or were I deaf, thy outward parts would move
Each part in me that were but sensible:
    Though neither eyes nor ears, to hear nor see,
    Yet should I be in love by touching thee.

"Say, that the sense of feeling were bereft me,
And that I could not see, nor hear, nor touch,
And nothing but the very smell were left me,
Yet would my love to thee be still as much;
    For from the stillitory of thy face excelling
    Comes breath perfumed, that breedeth love by
        smelling.

"But O, what banquet wert thou to the taste,
Being nurse and feeder of the other four!

Would they no; wish the feast might ever last,
And bid suspicion double-lock the door?
　　Lest Jealousy, that sour unwelcome guest,
　　Should, by his stealing in, disturb the feast."

Once more the ruby-colored portal opened,
Which to his speech did honey passage yield;
Like a red morn, that ever yet betokened
Wreck to the seaman, tempest to the field,
　　Sorrow to shepherds, woe unto the birds,
　　Gusts and foul flaws to herdmen and to herds.

This ill presage advisedly she marketh:
Even as the wind is hushed before it raineth,
Or as the wolf doth grin before he barketh,
Or as the berry breaks before it staineth,
　　Or like the deadly bullet of a gun,
　　His meaning struck her ere his words begun.

And at his look she flatly falleth down,
For looks kill love, and love by looks reviveth;
A smile recures the wounding of a frown;
But blessèd bankrupt, that by love so thriveth!
　　The silly boy, believing she is dead,
　　Claps her pale cheek, till clapping makes it red;

And all amazed brake off his late intent,
For sharply did he think to reprehend her,
Which cunning love did wittily prevent:
Fair fall the wit that can so well defend her!
　　For on the grass she lies as she were slain,
　　Till his breath breatheth life in her again.

He wrings her nose, he strikes her on the cheeks,
He bends her fingers, holds her pulses hard,
He chafes her lips; a thousand ways he seeks

To mend the hurt that his unkindness marred:
  He kisses her; and she, by her good will,
  Will never rise, so he will kiss her still.

The night of sorrow now is turned to day:
  Her two blue windows faintly she upheaveth,
  Like the fair sun, when in his fresh array
  He cheers the morn, and all the earth relieveth:
    And as the bright sun glorifies the sky,
    So is her face illumined with her eye;

Whose beams upon his hairless face are fixed,
  As if from thence they borrowed all their shine.
  Were never four such lamps together mixed,
  Had not his clouded with his brows' repine;
    But hers, which through the crystal tears gave
      light,
    Shone like the moon in water seen by night.

"O, where am I?" quoth she, "in earth or heaven,
  Or in the ocean drenched, or in the fire?
  What hour is this: or morn or weary even?
  Do I delight to die, or life desire?
    But now I lived, and life was death's annoy;
    But now I died, and death was lively joy.

"O, thou didst kill me, kill me once again:
  Thy eyes' shrewd tutor, that hard heart of thine,
  Hath taught them scornful tricks, and such disdain,
  That they have murdered this poor heart of mine;
    And these mine eyes, true leaders to their queen,
    But for thy piteous lips no more had seen.

"Long may they kiss each other, for this cure!
  O, never let their crimson liveries wear!
  And as they last, their verdure still endure,

To drive infection from the dangerous year!
  That the stargazers, having writ on death,
  May say, the plague is banished by thy breath.

"Pure lips, sweet seals in my soft lips imprinted,
What bargains may I make, still to be sealing?
To sell myself I can be well contented,
So thou wilt buy, and pay, and use good dealing;
  Which purchase if thou make, for fear of slips
  Set thy seal manual on my wax-red lips.

"A thousand kisses buys my heart from me;
And pay them at thy leisure, one by one.
What is ten hundred kisses unto thee?
Are they not quickly told, and quickly gone?
  Say, for non-payment that the debt should double,
  Is twenty hundred kisses such a trouble?"

"Fair queen," quoth he, "if any love you owe me,
Measure my strangeness with my unripe years;
Before I know myself, seek not to know me;
No fisher but the ungrown fry forbears:
  The mellow plum doth fall, the green sticks fast,
  Or being early plucked is sour to taste.

"Look, the world's comforter, with weary gait,
His day's hot task hath ended in the west:
The owl, night's herald, shrieks—'tis very late;
The sheep are gone to fold, birds to their nest;
  And coal-black clouds that shadow heaven's light
  Do summon us to part, and bid good night.

"Now let me say good night, and so say you;
If you will say so, you shall have a kiss."
"Good night" quoth she; and, ere he says "Adieu,"

The honey fee of parting tendered is:
   Her arms do lend his neck a sweet embrace
   Incorporate then they seem; face grows to face;

Till, breathless, he disjoined, and backward drew
The heavenly moisture, that sweet coral mouth,
Whose precious taste her thirsty lips well knew,
Whereon they surfeit, yet complain on drought:
   He with her plenty pressed, she faint with dearth,
   Their lips together glued, fall to the earth.

Now quick desire hath caught the yielding prey,
And glutton-like she feeds, yet never filleth;
Her lips are conquerors, his lips obey,
Paying what ransom the insulter willeth;
   Whose vulture thought doth pitch the price so high,
   That she will draw his lips' rich treasure dry.

And having felt the sweetness of the spoil,
With blindfold fury she begins to forage;
Her face doth reek and smoke, her blood doth boil,
And careless lust stirs up a desperate courage;
   Planting oblivion, beating reason back,
   Forgetting shame's pure blush and honor's wrack.

Hot, faint, and weary with her hard embracing,
Like a wild bird being tamed with too much handling,
Or as the fleet-foot roe that's tired with chasing,
Or like the froward infant stilled with dandling,
   He now obeys, and now no more resisteth,
   While she takes all she can, not all she listeth.

What wax so frozen but dissolves with tempering,
And yields at last to every light impression?
Things out of hope are compassed oft with venturing,

—33—

Chiefly in love, whose leave exceeds commission:
Affection faints not like a pale-faced coward,
But then woos best when most his choice is froward.

When he did frown, O, had she then gave over,
Such nectar from his lips she had not sucked.
Foul words and frowns must not repel a lover;
What though the rose have prickles, yet 'tis plucked:
    Were beauty under twenty locks kept fast,
    Yet love breaks through, and picks them all at last.

For pity now she can no more detain him;
The poor fool prays her that he may depart:
She is resolved no longer to restrain him;
Bids him farewell, and look well to her heart,
    The which, by Cupid's bow she doth protest,
    He carries thence incagèd in his breast.

"Sweet boy," she says, "this night I'll waste in sorrow,
For my sick heart commands mine eyes to watch.
Tell me, love's master, shall we meet tomorrow?
Say, shall we, shall we? Wilt thou make the match?"
    He tells her, no; tomorrow he intends
    To hunt the boar with certain of his friends.

"The boar!" quoth she; whereat a sudden pale,
Like lawn being spread upon the blushing rose,
Usurps her cheek; she trembles at his tale,
And on his neck her yoking arms she throws:
    She sinketh down, still hanging by his neck,
    He on her belly falls, she on her back.

Now she is in the very lists of love,
Her champion mounted for the hot encounter:
All is imaginary she doth prove,

He will not manage her, although he mount her;
  That worse than Tantalus' is her annoy,
  To clip Elysium, and to lack her joy.

Even as poor birds, deceived with painted grapes,
Do surfeit by the eye and pine the maw,
Even so she languisheth in her mishaps,
As those poor birds that helpless berries saw.
  The warm effects which she in him finds missing,
  She seeks to kindle with continual kissing.

But all in vain; good queen, it will not be:
She hath assayed as much as may be proved;
Her pleading hath deserved a greater fee;
She's Love, she loves, and yet she is not loved.
  "Fie, fie," he says, "you crush me; let me go;
  You have no reason to withhold me so."

"Thou hadst been gone," quoth she, "sweet boy, ere this,
But that thou told'st me thou wouldst hunt the boar.
O, be advised; thou know'st not what it is
With javelin's point a churlish swine to gore,
  Whose tushes never sheathed he whetteth still,
  Like to a mortal butcher, bent to kill.

"On his bow-back he hath a battle set
Of bristly pikes, that ever threat his foes;
His eyes like glowworms shine when he doth fret:
His snout digs sepulchers where'er he goes,
  Being moved, he strikes whate'er is in his way,
  And whom he strikes his cruel tushes slay.

"His brawny sides, with hairy bristles armed,
Are better proof than thy spear's point can enter;
His short thick neck cannot be easily harmed;

Being ireful on the lion he will venture:
  The thorny brambles and embracing bushes,
  As fearful of him, part; through whom he rushes.

"Alas, he naught esteems that face of thine,
To which Love's eyes pay tributary gazes;
Nor thy soft hands, sweet lips, and crystal eyne,
Whose full perfection all the world amazes;
  But having thee at vantage—wondrous dread!—
  Would root these beauties as he roots the mead.

"Oh, let him keep his loathsome cabin still!
Beauty hath naught to do with such foul fiends:
Come not within his danger by this will;
They that thrive well take counsel of their friends.
  When thou didst name the boar, not to dissemble,
  I feared thy fortune, and my joints did tremble.

"Didst thou not mark my face? Was it not white?
Saw'st thou not signs of fear lurk in mine eye?
Grew I not faint, and fell I not downright?
Within my bosom, whereon thou dost lie,
  My boding heart pants, beats, and takes no rest,
  But, like an earthquake, shakes thee on my breast.

"For where Love reigns, disturbing Jealousy
Doth call himself Affection's sentinel;
Gives false alarms, suggesteth mutiny,
And in a peaceful hour doth cry, 'Kill, kill!'
  Distemp'ring gentle Love in his desire,
  As air and water do abate the fire.

"This sour informer, this bate-breeding spy,
This canker that eats up Love's tender spring,
This carry-tale, dissentious Jealousy,

That sometime true news, sometime false doth bring,
  Knocks at my heart, and whispers in mine ear,
  That if I love thee, I thy death should fear:

"And more than so, presenteth to mine eye
The picture of an angry-chafing boar,
Under whose sharp fangs on his back doth lie
An image like thyself, all stained with gore;
  Whose blood upon the fresh flowers being shed
  Doth make them droop with grief and hang the head.

"What should I do, seeing thee so indeed,
That tremble at the imagination?
The thought of it doth make my faint heart bleed,
And fear doth teach it divination:
  I prophesy thy death, my living sorrow,
  If thou encounter with the boar tomorrow.

"But if thou needs will hunt, be ruled by me;
Uncouple at the timorous flying hare,
Or at the fox, which lives by subtlety,
Or at the roe, which no encounter dare:
  Pursue these fearful creatures o'er the downs,
  And on thy well-breathed horse keep with thy hounds.

"And when thou hast on foot the purblind hare,
Mark the poor wretch, to overshoot his troubles,
How he outruns the wind, and with what care
He cranks and crosses with a thousand doubles:
  The many musits through the which he goes
  Are like a labyrinth to amaze his foes.

"Sometime he runs among a flock of sheep,
To make the cunning hounds mistake their smell,
And sometime where earth-delving conies keep,

To stop the loud pursuers in their yell;
And sometime sorteth with a herd of deer:
Danger deviseth shifts; wit waits on fear:

"For there his smell with others being mingled,
The hot scent-snuffing hounds are driven to doubt,
Ceasing their clamorous cry till they have singled
With much ado the cold fault cleanly out;
    Then do they spend their mouths: Echo replies,
    As if another chase were in the skies.

"By this, poor Wat, far off upon a hill,
Stands on his hinder legs with listening ear,
To hearken if his foes pursue him still:
Anon their loud alarums he doth hear;
    And now his grief may be comparèd well
    To one sore sick that hears the passing bell.

"Then shalt thou see the dew-bedabbled wretch
Turn, and return, indenting with the way;
Each envious briar his weary legs doth scratch,
Each shadow makes him stop, each murmur stay:
    For misery is trodden on by many,
    And being low never relieved by any.

"Lie quietly, and hear a little more;
Nay, do not struggle, for thou shalt not risc:
To make thee hate the hunting of the boar,
Unlike myself thou hear'st me moralize,
    Applying this to that, and so to so;
    For love can comment upon every woe.

"Where did I leave?"—"No matter where," quoth he;
"Leave me, and then the story aptly ends:
The night is spent." "Why, what of that?" quoth she.

"I am," quoth he, "expected of my friends;
And now 'tis dark, and going I shall fall."
"In night," quoth she, "desire sees best of all.

"But if thou fall, O, then imagine this,
The earth in love with thee thy footing trips,
And all is but to rob thee of a kiss.
Rich preys make true men thieves; so do thy lips
    Make modest Dian cloudy and forlorn,
    Lest she should steal a kiss, and die forsworn.

"Now of this dark night I perceive the reason:
Cynthia for shame obscures her silver shine,
Till forging Nature be condemned of treason,
For stealing molds from heaven that were divine,
    Wherein she framed thee in high heaven's despite,
    To shame the sun by day, and her by night.

"And therefore hath she bribed the Destinies,
To cross the curious workmanship of nature,
To mingle beauty with infirmities,
And pure perfection with impure defeature;
    Making it subject to the tyranny
    Of mad mischances and much misery;

"As burning fevers, agues pale and faint,
Life-poisoning pestilence, and frenzies wood,
The marrow-eating sickness, whose attaint
Disorder breeds by heating of the blood:
    Surfeits, imposthumes, grief, and damned despair,
    Swear Nature's death for framing thee so fair.

"And not the least of all these maladies,
But in one minute's fight brings beauty under:
Both favor, savor, hue, and qualities,

Whereat th'impartial gazer late did wonder,
  Are on the sudden wasted, thawed, and done,
  As mountain snow melts with the midday sun.

"Therefore, despite of fruitless chastity,
Love-lacking vestals, and self-loving nuns,
That on the earth would breed a scarcity
And barren dearth of daughters and of sons,
  Be prodigal. The lamp that burns by night
  Dries up his oil to lend the world his light.

"What is thy body but a swallowing grave,
Seeming to bury that posterity
Which by the rights of time thou needs must have,
If thou destroy them not in dark obscurity?
  If so, the world will hold thee in disdain,
  Sith in thy pride so fair a hope is slain.

"So in thyself thyself art made away;
A mischief worse than civil, home-bred strife,
Or theirs whose desperate hands themselves do slay.
Or butcher sire, that reaves his son of life.
  Foul-cank'ring rust the hidden treasure frets,
  But gold that's put to use more gold begets."

"Nay, then," quoth Adon, "you will fail again
Into your idle over-handled theme:
The kiss I gave you is bestowed in vain,
And all in vain you strive against the stream;
  For by this black-faced night, desire's foul nurse,
  Your treatise makes me like you worse and worse.

"If love have lent you twenty thousand tongues,
And every tongue more moving than your own,
Bewitching like the wanton mermaid's songs,

Yet from mine ear the tempting tune is blown;
  For know, my heart stands armèd in mine ear,
  And will not let a false sound enter there;

"Lest the deceiving harmony should run
Into the quiet closure of my breast;
And then my little heart were quite undone,
In his bedchamber be barred of rest.
    No, lady, no; my heart longs not to groan,
    But soundly sleeps, while now it sleeps alone.

"What have you urged that I cannot reprove?
The path is smooth that leadeth on to danger;
I hate not love, but your device in love,
That lends embracements unto every stranger.
    You do it for increase; O, strange excuse,
    When reason is the bawd to lust's abuse!

"Call it not love, for Love to heaven is fled,
Since sweating Lust on earth usurped his name;
Under whose simple semblance he hath fed
Upon fresh beauty, blotting it with blame;
    Which the hot tyrant stains and soon bereaves,
    As caterpillars do the tender leaves.

"Love comforteth like sunshine after rain,
But Lust's effect is tempest after sun;
Love's gentle spring doth always fresh remain,
Lust's winter comes ere summer half be done.
    Love surfeits not; Lust like a glutton dies:
    Love is all truth; Lust full of forgèd lies.

"More I could tell, but more I dare not say;
The text is old, the orator too green:
Therefore, in sadness, now I will away;

My face is full of shame, my heart of teen;
  Mine ears that to your wanton talk attended
  Do burn themselves for having so offended."

With this, he breaketh from the sweet embrace
Of those fair arms which bound him to her breast,
And homeward through the dark laund runs apace;
Leaves Love upon her back deeply distressed.
  Look, how a bright star shooteth from the sky,
  So glides he in the night from Venus' eye;

Which after him she darts, as one on shore
Gazing upon a late-embarkèd friend,
Till the wild waves will have him seen no more,
Whose ridges with the meeting clouds contend;
  So did the merciless and pitchy night
  Fold in the object that did feed her sight.

Whereat amazed, as one that unaware
Hath dropped a precious jewel in the flood,
Or 'stonished as night wand'rers often are,
Their light blown out in some mistrustful wood;
  Even so confounded in the dark she lay,
  Having lost the fair discovery of her way.

And now she beats her heart, whereat it groans,
That all the neighbor caves, as seeming troubled,
Make verbal repetition of her moans;
Passion on passion deeply is redoubled:
  "Ah me," she cries, and twenty times, "Woe, woe!"
  And twenty echoes twenty times cry so.

She, marking them, begins a wailing note,
And sings extemporally a woeful ditty;
How love makes young men thrall, and old men dote;

How love is wise in folly, foolish-witty:
  Her heavy anthem still concludes in woe,
  And still the choir of echoes answer so.

Her song was tedious, and outwore the night,
For lovers' hours are long, though seeming short:
If pleased themselves, others, they think, delight
In such-like circumstances, with such-like sport:
  Their copious stories, oftentimes begun,
  End without audience, and are never done.

For who hath she to spend the night withal,
But idle, sounds-resembling parasites;
Like shrill-tongued tapsters answering every call,
Soothing the humor of fantastic wits?
  She says, " 'Tis so:" they answer all, " 'Tis so;"
  And would say after her, if she said "No."

Lo, here the gentle lark, weary of rest,
From his moist cabinet mounts up on high,
And wakes the morning, from whose silver breast
The sun ariseth in his majesty;
  Who doth the world so gloriously behold,
  That cedar tops and hills seem burnished gold.

Venus salutes him with this fair good-morrow—
"O, thou clear god, and patron of all light,
From whom each lamp and shining star doth borrow
The beauteous influence that makes him bright,
  There lives a son, that sucked an earthly mother,
  May lend thee light, as thou dost lend to other."

This said, she hasteth to a myrtle grove,
Musing the morning is so much o'erworn,
And yet she hears no tidings of her love:

She hearkens for his hounds and for his horn:
  Anon she hears them chant it lustily,
  And all in haste she coasteth to the cry.

And as she runs, the bushes in the way
Some catch her by the neck, some kiss her face,
Some twine about her thigh to make her stay;
She wildly breaketh from their strict embrace,
    Like a milch doe, whose swelling dugs do ache,
    Hasting to feed her fawn hid in some brake.

By this, she hears the hounds are at a bay;
Whereat she starts, like one that spies an adder
Wreathed up in fatal folds just in his way,
The fear whereof doth make him shake and shudder;
    Even so the timorous yelping of the hounds
    Appalls her senses, and her spirit confounds.

For now she knows it is no gentle chase,
But the blunt boar, rough bear, or lion proud,
Because the cry remaineth in one place,
Where fearfully the dogs exclaim aloud:
    Finding their enemy to be so curst,
    They all strain court'sy who shall cope him first.

This dismal cry rings sadly in her ear,
Through which it enters to surprise her heart;
Who, overcome by doubt and bloodless fear,
With cold-pale weakness numbs each feeling part:
    Like soldiers when their captain once doth yield,
    They basely fly, and dare not stay the field.

Thus stands she in a trembling ecstasy;
Till, cheering up her senses all dismayed,
She tells them 'tis a causeless fantasy,

And childish error, that they are afraid;
  Bids them leave quaking, bids them fear no more—
  And with that word she spied the hunted boar;

Whose frothy mouth, bepainted all with red,
Like milk and blood being mingled both together,
A second fear through all her sinews spread,
Which madly hurries her she knows not whither:
  This way she runs, and now she will no further,
  But back retires to rate the boar for murder.

A thousand spleens bear her a thousand ways;
She treads the path that she untreads again;
Her more than haste is mated with delays,
Like the proceedings of a drunken brain,
  Full of respects yet naught at all respecting,
  In hand with all things, naught at all effecting.

Here kenneled in a brake she finds a hound,
And asks the weary caitiff for his master;
And there another licking of his wound,
'Gainst venomed sores the only sovereign plaster;
  And here she meets another sadly scowling,
  To whom she speaks, and he replies with howling.

When he hath ceased his ill-resounding noise,
Another flap-mouthed mourner, black and grim,
Against the welkin volleys out his voice;
Another and another answer him,
  Clapping their proud tails to the ground below,
  Shaking their scratched ears, bleeding as they go.

Look, how the world's poor people are amazed
At apparitions, signs, and prodigies,
Whereon with fearful eyes they long have gazed,

Infusing them with dreadful prophecies;
  So she at these sad signs draws up her breath,
  And, sighing it again, exclaims on Death:

"Hard-favored tyrant, ugly, meager, lean,
Hateful divorce of love"—thus chides she Death—
"Grim-grinning ghost, earth's worm, what dost thou
      mean
To stifle beauty and to steal his breath,
  Who when he lived, his breath and beauty set
  Gloss on the rose, smell to the violet?

"If he be dead—O, not, it cannot be,
Seeing his beauty, thou shouldst strike at it!—
O yes, it may; thou hast no eyes to see,
But hatefully at random dost thou hit:
  Thy mark is feeble age; but thy false dart
  Mistakes that aim, and cleaves an infant's heart.

"Hadst thou but bid beware, then he had spoke,
And hearing him, thy power had lost his power.
The Destinies will curse thee for this stroke;
They bid thee crop a weed, thou pluck'st a flower:
  Love's golden arrow at him should have fled,
  And not Death's ebon dart, to strike him dead.

"Dost thou drink tears, that thou provok'st such
      weeping?
What may a heavy groan advantage thee?
Why hast thou cast into eternal sleeping
Those eyes that taught all other eyes to see?
  Now Nature cares not for thy mortal vigor,
  Since her best work is ruined with thy rigor."

Here overcome, as one full of despair,
She vailed her eyelids, who, like sluices, stopped

The crystal tide that from her two cheeks fair
In the sweet channel of her bosom dropped;
  But through the floodgates break the silver rain,
  And with his strong course opens them again.

O, how her eyes and tears did lend and borrow!
Her eyes seen in the tears, tears in her eye;
Both crystals, where they viewed each other's sorrow—
Sorrow that friendly sighs sought still to dry;
  But like a stormy day, now wind, now rain,
  Sighs dry her cheeks, tears make them wet again.

Variable passions throng her constant woe,
As striving who should best become her grief;
All entertained, each passion labors so,
That every present sorrow seemeth chief,
  But none is best; then join they all together,
  Like many clouds consulting for foul weather.

By this, far off she hears some huntsman hollo;
A nurse's song ne'er pleased her babe so well:
The dire imagination she did follow
This sound of hope doth labor to expel;
  For now reviving joy bids her rejoice,
  And flatters her it is Adonis' voice.

Whereat her tears began to turn their tide,
Being prisoned in her eye, like pearls in glass;
Yet sometimes fall an orient drop beside,
Which her cheek melts, as scorning it should pass,
  To wash the foul face of the sluttish ground,
  Who is but drunken when she seemeth drowned.

O, hard-believing love, how strange it seems
Not to believe, and yet too credulous!
Thy weal and woe are both of them extremes;

Despair and hope make thee ridiculous:
  The one doth flatter thee in thoughts unlikely,
  In likely thoughts the other kills thee quickly.

Now she unweaves the web that she hath wrought;
Adonis lives, and Death is not to blame;
It was not she that called him all to naught;
Now she adds honors to his hateful name;
  She clepes him king of graves, and grave for kings,
  Imperious supreme of all mortal things.

"No, no," quoth she, "sweet Death, I did but jest;
Yet pardon me, I felt a kind of fear
Whenas I met the boar, that bloody beast,
Which knows no pity, but is still severe;
  Then, gentle shadow—truth I must confess—
  I railed on thee, fearing my love's decease.

" 'Tis not my fault: the boar provoked my tongue;
Be wreaked on him, invisible commander;
'Tis he, foul creature, that hath done thee wrong;
I did but act, he's author of thy slander.
  Grief hath two tongues, and never woman yet,
  Could rule them both, without ten women's wit."

Thus, hoping that Adonis is alive,
Her rash suspect she doth extenuate;
And that his beauty may the better thrive,
With Death she humbly doth insinuate;
  Tells him of trophies, statues, tombs, and stories
  His victories, his triumphs, and his glories.

"O, Jove," quoth she, "how much a fool was I,
To be of such a weak and silly mind,
To wail his death who lives, and must not die

Till mutual overthrow of mortal kind!
  For he being dead, with him is beauty slain,
  And, beauty dead, black chaos comes again.

"Fie, fie, fond love, thou art so full of fear
As one with treasure laden, hemmed with thieves;
Trifles, unwitnessèd with eye or ear,
Thy coward heart with false bethinking grieves."
  Even at this word she hears a merry horn,
  Whereat she leaps that was but late forlorn.

As falcon to the lure, away she flies;
The grass stoops not, she treads on it so light;
And in her haste unfortunately spies
The foul boar's conquest on her fair delight;
  Which seen, her eyes, as murdered with the view,
  Like stars ashamed of day, themselves withdrew;

Or, as the snail, whose tender horns being hit,
Shrinks backward in his shelly cave with pain,
And there, all smothered up, in shade doth sit,
Long after fearing to creep forth again;
  So, at his bloody view, her eyes are fled
  Into the deep dark cabins of her head;

Where they resign their office and their light
To the disposing of her troubled brain;
Who bids them still consort with ugly night,
And never wound the heart with looks again;
  Who, like a king perplexèd in his throne,
  By their suggestion gives a deadly groan,

Whereat each tributary subject quakes;
As when the wind, imprisoned in the ground,
Struggling for passage, earth's foundation shakes,

Which with cold terror doth men's minds confound,
This mutiny each part doth so surprise,
That from their dark beds once more leap her eyes;

And, being opened, threw unwilling light
Upon the wide wound that the boar had trenched
In his soft flank; whose wonted lily white
With purple tears, that his wound wept, was drenched:
No flower was nigh, no grass, herb, leaf, or weed,
But stole his blood, and seemed with him to bleed.

This solemn sympathy poor Venus noteth;
Over one shoulder doth she hang her head;
Dumbly she passions, franticly she doteth;
She thinks he could not die, he is not dead:
Her voice is stopped, her joints forget to bow;
Her eyes are mad that they have wept till now.

Upon his hurt she looks so steadfastly
That her sight dazzling makes the wound seem three;
And then she reprehends her mangling eye
That makes more gashes where no breach should be:
His face seems twain, each several limb is doubled;
For oft the eye mistakes, the brain being troubled.

"My tongue cannot express my grief for one,
And yet," quoth she, "behold two Adons dead!
My sighs are blown away, my salt tears gone,
Mine eyes are turned to fire, my heart to lead:
Heavy heart's lead melt at mine eyes' red fire!
So shall I die by drops of hot desire.

"Alas, poor world, what treasure has thou lost!
What face remains alive that's worth the viewing?
Whose tongue is music now? What canst thou boast

Of things long since, or anything ensuing?
  The flowers are sweet, their colors fresh and trim;
  But true-sweet beauty lived and died with him.

"Bonnet nor veil henceforth no creature wear!
Nor sun nor wind will ever strive to kiss you:
Having no fair to lose, you need not fear;
The sun doth scorn you, and the wind doth hiss you:
  But when Adonis lived, sun and sharp air
  Lurked like two thieves to rob him of his fair,

"And therefore would he put his bonnet on,
Under whose brim the gaudy sun would peep;
The wind would blow it off, and, being gone,
Play with his locks; then would Adonis weep;
  And straight, in pity of his tender years,
  They both would strive who first should dry his tears.

"To see his face the lion walked along
Behind some hedge, because he would not fear him;
To recreate himself, when he hath sung,
The tiger would be tame, and gently hear him;
  If he had spoke, the wolf would leave his prey,
  And never fright the silly lamb that day.

"When he beheld his shadow in the brook,
The fishes spread on it their golden gills;
When he was by, the birds such pleasure took,
That some would sing, some other in their bills
  Would bring him mulberries and ripe-red cherries.
  He fed them with his sight, they him with berries.

"But this foul, grim, and urchin-snouted boar,
Whose downward eye still looketh for a grave,
Ne'er saw the beauteous livery that he wore;

Witness the entertainment that he gave;
  If he did see his face, why then I know
  He thought to kiss him, and hath killed him so.

" 'Tis true, 'tis true; thus was Adonis slain:
He ran upon the boar with his sharp spear,
Who did not whet his teeth at him again,
But by a kiss thought to persuade him there;
  And nuzzling in his flank, the loving swine
  Sheathed, unaware, the tusk in his soft groin.

"Had I been toothed like him, I must confess,
With kissing him I should have killed him first;
But he is dead, and never did he bless
My youth with his—the more am I accursed."
  With this, she falleth in the place she stood,
  And stains her face with his congealèd blood.

She looks upon his lips, and they are pale;
She takes him by the hand, and that is cold;
She whispers in his ears a heavy tale,
As if they heard the woeful words she told;
  She lifts the coffer-lids that close his eyes,
  Where, lo, two lamps, burnt out, in darkness lies!

Two glasses, where herself herself beheld
A thousand times, and now no more reflect;
Their virtue lost, wherein they late excelled,
And every beauty robbed of his effect:
  "Wonder of time," quoth she, "this is my spite,
  That, thou being dead, the day should yet be light.

"Since thou art dead, lo, here I prophesy,
Sorrow on love hereafter shall attend!
It shall be waited on with jealousy,

Find sweet beginning, but unsavory end;
   Ne'er settled equally, but high or low;
   That all love's pleasure shall not match his woe.

"It shall be fickle, false, and full of fraud;
Bud and be blasted in a breathing-while;
The bottom poison, and the top o'erstrawed
With sweets that shall the truest sight beguile:
   The strongest body shall it make most weak,
   Strike the wise dumb, and teach the fool to speak.

"It shall be sparing, and too full of riot;
Teaching decrepit age to tread the measures,
The staring ruffian shall it keep in quiet;
Pluck down the rich, enrich the poor with treasures;
   It shall be raging-mad, and silly-mild,
   Make the young old, the old become a child.

"It shall suspect where there is no cause of fear;
It shall not fear where it should most mistrust;
It shall be merciful, and too severe,
And most deceiving when it seems most just;
   Perverse it shall be where it shows most toward,
   Put fear to valor, courage to the coward.

"It shall be cause of war and dire events,
And set dissention 'twixt the son and sire;
Subject and servile to all discontents,
As dry combustious matter is to fire;
   Sith in his prime death doth my love destroy,
   They that love best their loves shall not enjoy."

By this, the boy that by her side lay killed
Was melted like a vapor from her sight,
And in his blood, that on the ground lay spilled,

A purple flower sprung up, chequered with white,
  Resembling well his pale cheeks, and the blood
  Which in round drops upon their whiteness stood.

She bows her head, the new-sprung flower to smell,
Comparing it to her Adonis' breath;
And says, within her bosom it shall dwell,
Since he himself is reft from her by death:
  She crops the stalk, and in the breach appears
  Green-dropping sap, which she compares to tears.

"Poor flower," quoth she, "this was thy father's guise—
Sweet issue of a more sweet-smelling sire—
For every little grief to wet his eyes:
To grow unto himself was his desire,
  And so 'tis thine; hut know, it is as good
  To wither in my breast as in his blood.

"Here was thy father's bed, here in my breast;
Thou art the next of blood, and 'tis thy right:
Lo, in this hollow cradle take thy rest,
My throbbing heart shall rock thee day and night!
  There shall not be one minute in an hour
  Wherein I will not kiss my sweet love's flower."

Thus weary of the world, away she hies,
And yokes her silver doves; by whose swift aid
Their mistress, mounted, through the empty skies
In her light chariot quickly is conveyed;
  Holding their course to Paphos, where their queen
  Means to immure herself and not be seen.

The Rape
of Lucrece

TO THE RIGHT HONORABLE HENRY WRIOTHESLY,
EARL OF SOUTHAMPTON, AND BARON OF TICHFIELD

The love I dedicate to your Lordship is without end; whereof this pamphlet, without beginning, is but a superfluous moiety. The warrant I have of your honorable disposition, not the worth of my untutored lines, makes it assured of acceptance. What I have done is yours; what I have to do is yours; being part in all I have devoted yours. Were my worth greater, my duty would show greater; meantime, as it is, it is bound to your Lordship, to whom I wish long life, still lengthened with all happiness.

Your Lordship's in all duty,
William Shakespeare

THE ARGUMENT

Lucius Tarquinius—for his excessive pride surnamed Superbus—after he had caused his own father-in-law, Servius Tullius, to be cruelly murdered, and, contrary to the Roman laws and customs, not requiring or staying for the people's suffrages, had possessed himself of the kingdom, went, accompanied with his sons and other noblemen of Rome, to besiege Ardea. During which siege the principal men of the army meeting one evening at the tent of Sextus Tarquinius, the king's son, in their discourses after supper, everyone commended the virtues of his own wife; among whom, Collatinus extolled the incomparable chastity of his wife Lucretia. In that pleasant humor they all posted to Rome; and intending, by their secret and sudden arrival, to make trial of that which everyone had before avouched, only Collatinus finds his wife (though it were late in the night) spinning amongst her maids: the other ladies were all found dancing and revelling, or in several disports. Whereupon the noblemen yielded Collatinus the victory, and his wife the fame. At that time Sextus Tarquinius, being inflamed with Lucrece's beauty, yet smothering his passions for the present, departed with the rest back to the camp; from whence he shortly after privily withdrew himself, and was (according to his estate) royally entertained and lodged by Lucrece at Collatium. The same night he treacherously stealeth into her chamber, violently ravished her, and early in the morning speedeth away. Lucrece, in this lamentable plight, hastily dispatcheth messengers, one to Rome for her father, another to the camp for Collatine. They came, the one accompanied with Junius Brutus, the other with Publius Valerius; and finding Lucrece attired in mourning habit, demanded the cause of her sorrow. She, first taking an oath of them for her revenge, revealed the actor, and whole manner of his dealing, and withal suddenly stabbed herself. Which done, with one consent they all vowed to root out the whole hated family of the Tarquins; and bearing the dead body to Rome, Brutus acquainted the people with the doer and manner of the vile deed, with a bitter invective against the tyranny of the king; wherewith the people were so moved, that with one consent and a general acclamation, the Tarquins were all exiled, and the state government changed from kings to consuls.

THE RAPE
OF LUCRECE

From the besieged Ardea all in post,
Borne by the trustless wings of false desire,
Lust-breathèd Tarquin leaves the Roman host,
And to Collatium bears the lightless fire
Which, in pale embers hid, lurks to aspire,
    And girdle with embracing flames the waist
    Of Collatine's fair love, Lucrece the chaste.

Haply that name of "chaste" unhapp'ly set
This bateless edge on his keen appetite;
When Collatine unwisely did not let
To praise the clear unmatchèd red and white
Which triumphed in that sky of his delight,
    Where mortal stars, as bright as heaven's beauties
    With pure aspects did him peculiar duties.

For he the night before, in Tarquin's tent,
Unlocked the treasure of his happy state;
What priceless wealth the heavens had him lent
In the possession of his beauteous mate;
Reck'ning his fortune at such high-proud rate,
    That kings might be espousèd to more fame,
    But king nor peer to such a peerless dame.

O, happiness enjoyed but of a few!
And, if possessed, as soon decayed and done
As is the morning's silver melting dew
Against the golden splendor of the sun!
An expired date, canceled ere well begun:
    Honor and beauty, in the owner's arms,
    Are weakly fortressed from a world of harms.

Beauty itself doth of itself persuade
The eyes of men without an orator;
What needeth, then, apologies be made
To set forth that which is so singular?
Or why is Collatine the publisher
    Of that rich jewel he should keep unknown
    From thievish ears, because it is his own?

Perchance his boast of Lucrece' sov'reignty
Suggested this proud issue of a king;
For by our ears our hearts oft tainted be:
Perchance that envy of so rich a thing,
Braving compare, disdainfully did sting
    His high-pitched thoughts, that meaner men should
      vaunt
    That golden hap which their superiors want.

But some untimely thought did instigate
His all-too-timeless speed, if none of those:
His honor, his affairs, his friends, his state,
Neglected all, with swift intent he goes
To quench the coal which in his liver glows.
    O rash false heat, wrapped in repentant cold,
    Thy hasty spring still blasts, and ne'er grows old!

When at Collatium this false lord arrived,
Well was he welcomed by the Roman dame,
Within whose face beauty and virtue strived
Which of them both should underprop her fame:
When virtue bragged, beauty would blush for shame;
    When beauty boasted blushes, in despite
    Virtue would stain that or with silver white.

But beauty, in that white intitulèd,
From Venus' doves doth challenge that fair field:

Then virtue claims from beauty beauty's red,
Which virtue gave the golden age to gild
Their silver cheeks, and called it then their shield;
 Teaching them thus to use it in the fight—
 When shame assailed, the red should fence the
  white.

This heraldry in Lucrece' face was seen,
Argued by beauty's red and virtue's white:
Of either's color was the other queen,
Proving from world's minority their right:
Yet their ambition makes them still to fight;
 The sovereignty of either being so great,
 That oft they interchange each other's seat.

This silent war of lilies and of roses
Which Tarquin viewed in her fair face's field,
In their pure ranks his traitor eye encloses;
Where, lest between them both it should be killed,
The coward captive vanquishèd doth yield
 To those two armies that would let him go,
 Rather than triumph in so false a foe.

Now thinks he that her husband's shallow tongue—
The niggard prodigal that praised her so—
In that high task hath done her beauty wrong,
Which far exceeds his barren skill to show:
Therefore that praise which Collatine doth owe,
 Enchanted Tarquin answers with surmise,
 In silent wonder of still-gazing eyes.

This earthly saint, adorèd by this devil,
Little suspecteth the false worshipper;
For unstained thoughts do seldom dream on evil;
Birds never limed no secret bushes fear:

So guiltless she securely gives good cheer
  And reverend welcome to her princely guest
  Whose inward ill no outward harm expressed:

For that he colored with his high estate,
Hiding base sin in pleats of majesty;
That nothing in him seemed inordinate,
Save sometime too much wonder of his eye,
Which, having all, all could not satisfy;
  But poorly rich, so wanteth in his store,
  That, cloyed with much, he pineth still for more.

But she, that never coped with stranger eyes,
Could pick no meaning from their parling looks,
Nor read the subtle shining secrecies
Writ in the glassy margents of such books:
She touched no unknown baits, nor feared no hooks;
  Nor could she moralize his wanton sight
  More than his eyes were opened to the light.

He stories to her ears her husband's fame,
Won in the fields of fruitful Italy;
And decks with praises Collatine's high name,
Made glorious by his manly chivalry
With bruisèd arms and wreaths of victory:
  Her joy with heaved-up hand she doth express,
  And, wordless, so greets heaven for his success.

Far from the purpose of his coming thither,
He makes excuses for his being there.
No cloudy show of stormy blust'ring weather
Doth yet in his fair welkin once appear;
Till sable Night, mother of Dread and Fear,
  Upon the world dim darkness doth display,
  And in her vaulty prison stows the Day.

For then is Tarquin brought unto his bed,
Intending weariness with heavy sprite;
For, after supper, long he questionèd
With modest Lucrece, and wore out the night:
Now leaden slumber with life's strength doth fight;
    And everyone to rest themselves betake,
    Save thieves, and cares, and troubled minds, that
        wakes.

As one of which doth Tarquin lie revolving
The sundry dangers of his will's obtaining;
Yet ever to obtain his will resolving,
Though weak-built hopes persuade him to abstaining;
Despair to gain doth traffic oft for gaining;
    And when great treasure is the meed proposed,
    Though death be adjunct, there's no death supposed.

Those that much covet are with gain so fond,
That what they have not, that which they possess,
They scatter and unloose it from their bond,
And so, by hoping more, they have but less;
Or, gaining more, the profit of excess
    Is but to surfeit, and such griefs sustain,
    That they prove bankrupt in this poor-rich gain.

The aim of all is but to nurse the life
With honor, wealth, and ease, in waning age;
And in this aim there is such thwarting strife,
That one for all, or all for one we gage:
As life for honor in fell battles' rage,
    Honor for wealth; and oft that wealth doth cost
    The death of all, and all together lost.

So that in vent'ring ill we leave to be
The things we are for that which we expect;

And this ambitious-foul infirmity,
In having much, torments us with defect
Of that we have: so then we do neglect
   The thing we have, and, all for want of wit,
   Make something nothing by augmenting it.

Such hazard now must doting Tarquin make,
Pawning his honor to obtain his lust;
And for himself himself he must forsake:
Then where is truth, if there be no self-trust?
When shall he think to find a stranger just,
   When he himself himself confounds, betrays
   To sland'rous tongues and wretched hateful days?

Now stole upon the time the dead of night,
When heavy sleep had closed up mortal eyes:
No comfortable star did lend his light,
No noise but owls' and wolves' death-boding cries;
Now serves the season that they may surprise
   The silly lambs: pure thoughts are dead and still,
   While lust and murder wake to stain and kill.

And now this lustful lord leaped from his bed,
Throwing his mantle rudely o'er his arm;
Is madly tossed between desire and dread;
Th'one sweetly flatters, th'other feareth harm;
But honest Fear, bewitched with lust's foul charm,
   Doth too-too oft betake him to retire,
   Beaten away by brainsick rude Desire.

His falchion on a flint he softly smiteth,
That from the cold stone sparks of fire do fly,
Whereat a waxen torch forthwith he lighteth,
Which must be lodestar to his lustful eye;
And to the flame thus speaks advisedly,

"As from this cold flint I enforced this fire,
So Lucrece must I force to my desire."

Here pale with fear he doth premeditate
The dangers of his loathsome enterprise,
And in his inward mind he doth debate
What following sorrow may on this arise;
Then looking scornfully, he doth despise
    His naked armor of still-slaughtered lust,
    And justly thus controls his thoughts unjust:

"Fair torch, burn out thy light, and lend it not
To darken her whose light excelleth thine!
And die, unhallowed thoughts, before you blot
With your uncleanness that which is divine!
Offer pure incense to so pure a shrine:
    Let fair humanity abhor the deed
    That spots and stains love's modest snow-white
        weed.

"O shame to knighthood and to shining arms!
O foul dishonor to my household's graves
O impious act, including all foul harms!
A martial man to be soft fancy's slave
True valor still a true respect should have;
    Then my digression is so vile, so base,
    That it will live engraven in my face.

"Yea, though I die, the scandal will survive,
And be an eyesore in my golden coat;
Some loathsome dash the herald will contrive,
To cipher me how fondly I did dote;
That my posterity, shamed with the note,
    Shall curse my bones, and hold it for no sin
    To wish that I their father had not been.

"What win I, if I gain the thing I seek?
A dream, a breath, a froth of fleeting joy.
Who buys a minute's mirth to wail a week?
Or sells eternity to get a toy?
For one sweet grape who will the vine destroy?
    Or what fond beggar, but to touch the crown,
    Would with the scepter straight be strucken
        down?

"If Collatinus dream of my intent,
Will he not wake, and in a desp'rate rage
Post hither, this vile purpose to prevent?
This siege that hath engirt his marriage,
This blur to youth, this sorrow to the sage,
    This dying virtue, this surviving shame,
    Whose crime will bear an ever-during blame?

"O, what excuse can my invention make,
When thou shalt charge me with so black a deed?
Will not my tongue be mute, my frail joints shake,
Mine eyes forego their light, my false heart bleed?
The guilt being great, the fear doth still exceed;
    And extreme fear can neither fight nor fly,
    But coward-like with trembling terror die.

"Had Collatinus killed my son or sire,
Or lain in ambush to betray my life,
Or were he not my dear friend, this desire
Might have excuse to work upon his wife,
As in revenge or quittal of such strife:
    But as he is my kinsman, my dear friend,
    The shame and fault finds no excuse nor end.

"Shameful it is—ay, if the fact be known:
Hateful it is—there is no hate in loving:

I'll beg her love—but she is not her own:
The worst is but denial and reproving:
My will is strong, past reason's weak removing
  Who fears a sentence or an old man's saw
  Shall by a painted cloth be kept in awe."

Thus, graceless, holds he disputation
'Tween frozen conscience and hot-burning will,
And with good thoughts makes dispensation,
Urging the worser sense for vantage still;
Which in a moment doth confound and kill
  All pure effects, and doth so far proceed,
  That what is vile shows like a virtuous deed.

Quoth he, "She took me kindly by the hand,
And gaz'd for tidings in my eager eyes,
Fearing some hard news from the warlike band
Where her belovèd Collatinus lies.
O, how her fear did make her color rise!
  First red as roses that on lawn we lay,
  Then white as lawn, the roses took away.

"And how her hand, in my hand being locked,
Forced it to tremble with her loyal fear!
Which struck her sad, and then it faster rocked,
Until her husband's welfare she did hear;
Whereat she smilèd with so sweet a cheer,
  That had Narcissus seen her as she stood,
  Self-love had never drowned him in the flood.

"Why hunt I, then, for color or excuses?
All orators are dumb when beauty pleadeth;
Poor wretches have remorse in poor abuses;
Love thrives not in the heart that shadows
    dreadeth:

Affection is my captain, and he leadeth;
And when his gaudy banner is displayed,
The coward fights, and will not be dismayed.

"Then, childish fear, avaunt, debating, die!
Respect and reason, wait on wrinkled age!
My heart shall never countermand mine eye:
Sad pause and deep regard beseem the sage;
My part is youth, and beats these from the stage:
    Desire my pilot is, beauty my prize;
    Then who fears sinking where such treasure lies?"

As corn o'ergrown by weeds, so heedful fear
Is almost choked by unresisted lust.
Away he steals with open list'ning ear,
Full of foul hope, and full of fond mistrust;
Both which, as servitors to the unjust,
    So cross him with their opposite persuasion,
    That now he vows a league, and now invasion.

Within his thought her heavenly image sits,
And in the selfsame seat sits Collatine:
That eye which looks on her confounds his wits;
That eye which him beholds, as more divine,
Unto a view so false will not incline;
    But with a pure appeal seeks to the heart,
    Which once corrupted takes the worser part;

And therein heartens up his servile powers,
Who, flattered by their leader's jocund show,
Stuff up his lust, as minutes fill up hours;
And as their captain, so their pride doth grow,
Paying more slavish tribute than they owe.
    By reprobate desire thus madly led,
    The Roman lord marcheth to Lucrece' bed.

The locks between her chamber and his will,
Each one by him enforced, retires his ward;
But, as they open, they all rate his ill,
Which drives the creeping thief to some regard;
The threshold grates the door to have him heard;
    Night-wand'ring weasels shriek to see him there;
    They fright him, yet he still pursues his fear.

As each unwilling portal yields him way,
Through little vents and crannies of the place
The wind wars with his torch to make him stay,
And blows the smoke of it into his face,
Extinguishing his conduct in this case;
    But his hot heart, which fond desire doth scorch,
    Puffs forth another wind that fires the torch;

And being lighted, by the light he spies
Lucretia's glove, wherein her needle sticks:
He takes it from the rushes where it lies,
And gripping it, the needle his finger pricks:
As who should say, "This glove to wanton tricks
    Is not inured; return again in haste;
    Thou see'st our mistress' ornaments are chaste."

But all these poor forbiddings could not stay him;
He in the worst sense construes their denial:
The doors, the wind, the glove, that did delay him,
He takes for accidental things of trial;
Or as those bars which stop the hourly dial,
    Who with a ling'ring stay his course doth let,
    Till every minute pays the hour his debt.

"So, so," quoth he, "these lets attend the time,
Like little frosts that sometime threat the spring,
To add a more rejoicing to the prime,

And give the sneapèd birds more cause to sing.
Pain pays the income of each precious thing;
   Huge rocks, high winds, strong pirates, shelves
      and sands,
   The merchant fear, ere rich at home he lands."

Now is he come unto the chamber door,
That shuts him from the heaven of his thought,
Which with a yielding latch, and with no more,
Hath barred him from the blessèd thing he sought.
So from himself impiety hath wrought,
   That for his prey to pray he doth begin,
   As if the heavens should countenance his sin.

But in the midst of his unfruitful prayer,
Having solicited th'eternal power,
That his foul thoughts might compass his fair fair,
And they would stand auspicious to the hour,
Even there he starts—quoth he, "I must deflower:
   The powers to whom I pray abhor this fact,
   How can they, then, assist me in the act?

"Then Love and Fortune be my gods, my guide!
My will is backed with resolution:
Thoughts are but dreams till their effects be tried;
The blackest sin is cleared with absolution;
Against love's fire fear's frost hath dissolution.
   The eye of heaven is out, and misty night
   Covers the shame that follows sweet delight,"

This said, his guilty hand plucked up the latch,
And with his knee the door he opens wide.
The dove sleeps fast that this night owl will catch:
Thus treason works ere traitors be espied.
Who sees the lurking serpent steps aside;

But she, sound sleeping, fearing no such thing,
Lies at the mercy of his mortal sting.

Into the chamber wickedly he stalks,
And gazeth on her yet-unstainèd bed.
The curtains being close, about he walks,
Rolling his greedy eyeballs is his head:
By their high treason in his heart misled;
    Which gives the watchword to his hands full soon,
    To draw the cloud that hides the silver moon.

Look, as the fair and fiery-pointed sun,
Rushing from forth a cloud, bereaves our sight;
Even so, the curtain drawn, his eyes begun
To wink, being blinded with a greater light:
Whether it is that she reflects so bright.
    That dazzleth them, or else some shame supposed;
    But blind they are, and keep themselves enclosed.

O, had they in that darksome prison died!
Then had they seen the period of their ill;
Then Collatine again, by Lucrece' side,
In his clear bed might have reposèd still:
But they must ope, this blessèd league to kill;
    And holy-thoughted Lucrece to their sight
    Must sell her joy, her life, her world's delight.

Her lily hand her rosy cheek lies under,
Coz'ning the pillow of a lawful kiss;
Who, therefore angry, seems to part in sunder,
Swelling on either side to want his bliss;
Between whose hills her head entombèd is:
    Where, like a virtuous monument, she lies,
    To be admired of lewd unhallowed eyes.

Without the bed her other fair hand was,
On the green coverlet; whose perfect white
Showed like an April daisy on the grass,
With pearly sweat, resembling dew of night.
Her eyes, like marigolds, had sheathed their light,
   And canopied in darkness sweetly lay,
   Till they might open to adorn the day.

Her hair, like golden threads, played with her breath;
O modest wantons! wanton modesty!
Showing life's triumph in the map of death,
And death's dim look in life's mortality:
Each in her sleep themselves so beautify,
   As if between them twain there were no strife,
   But that life lived in death, and death in life.

Her breasts, like ivory globes circled with blue,
A pair of maiden worlds unconquerèd,
Save of their lord no bearing yoke they knew,
And him by oath they truly honorèd.
These worlds in Tarquin new ambition bred;
   Who, like a foul usurper, went about
   From this fair throne to heave the owner out.

What could he see, but mightily he noted?
What did he note, but strongly he desired?
What he beheld, on that he firmly doted,
And in his will his willful eye he tired.
With more than admiration he admired
   Her azure veins, her alabaster skin,
   Her coral lips, her snow-white dimpled chin.

As the grim lion fawneth o'er his prey,
Sharp hunger by the conquest satisfied,

So o'er this sleeping soul doth Tarquin stay,
His rage of lust by gazing qualified;
Slacked, not suppressed; for standing by her side,
  His eye, which late this mutiny restrains,
  Unto a greater uproar tempts his veins:

And they, like straggling slaves for pillage fighting,
Obdurate vassals fell exploits effecting,
In bloody death and ravishment delighting,
Nor children's tears nor mothers' groans respecting,
  Swell in their pride, the onset still expecting:
    Anon his beating heart, alarum striking,
    Gives the hot charge, and bids them do their liking.

His drumming heart cheers up his burning eye,
His eye commends the leading to his hand;
His hand, as proud of such a dignity,
Smoking with pride, marched on to make his stand
On her bare breast, the heart of all her land;
  Whose ranks of blue veins, as his hand did scale,
  Left their round turrets destitute and pale.

They, must'ring to the quiet cabinet
Where their dear governess and lady lies,
Do tell her she is dreadfully beset,
And fright with confusion of their cries:
She, much amazed, breaks ope her locked-up eyes,
  Who, peeping forth this tumult to behold,
  Are by his flaming torch dimmed and controlled.

Imagine her as one in dead of night
From forth dull sleep by dreadful fancy waking,
That thinks she hath beheld some ghastly sprite,
Whose grim aspect sets every joint a-shaking;

What terror 'tis! but she, in worser taking,
From sleep disturbèd, heedfully doth view
The sight which makes supposèd terror true.

Wrapped and confounded in a thousand fears,
Like to a new-killed bird she trembling lies;
She does not look; yet, winking, there appears
Quick-shifting antics, ugly in her eyes:
Such shadows are the weak brain's forgeries:
    Who, angry that the eyes fly from their lights,
    In darkness haunts them with more dreadful sights.

His hand, that yet remains upon her breast—
Rude ram, to batter such an ivory wall!—
May feel her heart—(poor citizen!) distressed,
Wounding itself to death, rise up and fall,
Beating her bulk, that his hand shakes withal.
    This moves in him more rage, and lesser pity,
    To make the breach, and enter this sweet city.

First, like a trumpet, doth his tongue begin
To sound a parley to his heartless foe;
Who o'er the white sheet peers her whiter chin,
The reason of this rash alarm to know,
Which he by dumb demeanor seeks to show;
    But she with vehement prayers urgeth still
    Under what color he commits this ill.

Thus he replies: "The color in thy face—
That even for anger makes the lily pale,
And the red rose blush at her own disgrace—
Shall plead for me, and tell my loving tale:
Under that color am I come to scale
    Thy never-conquered fort; the fault is thine,
    For those thine eyes betray thee unto mine.

"Thus I forestall thee, if thou mean to chide:
Thy beauty hath ensnared thee to this night,
Where thou with patience must my will abide;
My will that marks thee for my earth's delight,
Which I to conquer sought with all my might;
    But as reproof and reason beat it dead,
    By thy bright beauty was it newly bred.

"I see what crosses my attempt will bring;
I know what thorns the growing rose defends;
I think the honey guarded with a sting;
All this, beforehand, counsel comprehends:
But will is deaf, and hears no heedful friends;
    Only he hath an eye to gaze on beauty,
    And dotes on what he looks, 'gainst law or duty.

"I have debated, even in my soul,
What wrong, what shame, what sorrow I shall breed;
But nothing can affection's course control,
Or stop the headlong fury of his speed.
I know repentant tears ensue the deed,
    Reproach, disdain, and deadly enmity;
    Yet strive I to embrace mine infamy."

This said, he shakes aloft his Roman blade,
Which, like a falcon tow'ring in the skies
Coucheth the fowl below with his wings' shade,
Whose crooked beak threats if he mount he dies:
So under his insulting falchion lies
    Harmless Lucretia, marking what he tells,
    With trembling fear, as fowl hear falcon's bells.

"Lucrece," quoth he, "this night I must enjoy thee:
If thou deny, then force must work my way,
For in thy bed I purpose to destroy thee;

That done, some worthless slave of thine I'll slay,
To kill thine honor with thy life's decay;
    And in thy dead arms do I mean to place him,
    Swearing I slew him, seeing thee embrace him.

"So thy surviving husband shall remain
The scornful mark of every open eye;
Thy kinsmen hang their heads at this disdain,
Thy issue blurred with nameless bastardy:
And thou, the author of their obloquy,
    Shalt have thy trespass cited up in rhymes,
    And sung by children in succeeding times.

"But if thou yield, I rest thy secret friend:
The fault unknown is as a thought unacted;
A little harm, done to a great good end,
For lawful policy remains enacted.
The poisonous simple sometime is compacted
    In a pure compound; being so applied,
    His venom in effect is purified.

"Then, for thy husband and thy children's sake,
Tender my suit: bequeath not to their lot
The shame that from them no device can take,
The blemish that will never be forgot;
Worse than a slavish wipe, or birth-hour's blot:
    For marks descried in men's nativity
    Are nature's faults, not their own infamy."

Here with a cockatrice' dead-killing eye
He rouseth up himself, and makes a pause;
While she, the picture of pure piety,
Like a white hind under the grype's sharp claws,
Pleads, in a wilderness, where are no laws,

To the rough beast that knows no gentle right,
Nor aught obeys but his foul appetite.

But when a black-faced cloud the world doth threat,
In his dim mist th'aspiring mountains hiding,
From earth's dark womb some gentle gust doth get,
Which blows these pitchy vapors from their biding,
Hind'ring their present fall by this dividing;
    So his unhallowed haste her words delays,
    And moody Pluto winks while Orphous plays.

Yet, foul night-waking cat, he doth but dally,
While in his holdfast foot the weak mouse panteth;
Her sad behavior feeds his vulture folly,
A swallowing gulf that even in plenty wanteth:
His ear her prayers admits, but his heart granteth
    No penetrable entrance to her plaining:
    Tears harden lust, though marble wear with raining.

Her pity-pleading eyes are sadly fixed
In the remorseless wrinkles of his face;
Her modest eloquence with sighs is mixed,
Which to her oratory adds more grace.
She puts the period often from his place,
    And midst the sentence so her accent breaks,
    That twice she doth begin ere once she speaks.

She conjures him by high almighty Jove,
By knighthood, gentry, and sweet friendship's oath,
By her untimely tears, her husband's love,
By holy human law, and common troth,
By heaven and earth, and all the power of both,
    That to his borrowed bed he make retire,
    And stoop to honor, not to foul desire.

Quoth she, "Reward not hospitality
With such black payment as thou hast pretended;
Mud not the fountain that gave drink to thee;
Mar not the thing that cannot be amended;
End thy ill aim before thy shoot be ended:
    He is no woodman that doth bend his bow
    To strike a poor unseasonable doe.

"My husband is thy friend—for his sake spare me;
Thyself art mighty—for thine own sake leave me;
Myself a weakling—do not, then, ensnare me;
Thou look'st not like deceit—do not deceive me.
My sighs, like whirlwinds, labor hence to heave thee:
    If ever man were moved with woman's moans,
    Be movèd with my tears, my sighs, my groans:

"All which together, like a troubled ocean,
Beat at thy rocky and wreck-threat'ning heart,
To soften it with their continual motion;
For stones dissolved to water do convert.
O, if no harder than a stone thou art,
    Melt at my tears, and be compassionate!
    Soft pity enters at an iron gate.

"In Tarquin's likeness I did entertain thee;
Hast thou put on his shape to do him shame?
To all the host of heaven I complain me,
Thou wrong'st his honor, wound'st his princely name.
Thou art not what thou seem'st; and if the same,
    Thou seem'st not what thou art, a god, a king;
    For kings like gods should govern everything.

"How will thy shame be seeded in thine age,
When thus thy vices bud before thy spring?

If in thy hope thou dar'st do such outrage,
What dar'st thou not when once thou art a king?
O, be remembered, no outrageous thing
    From vassal actors can be wiped away;
    Then kings' misdeeds cannot be hid in clay.

"This deed will make thee only loved for fear;
But happy monarchs still are feared for love:
With foul offenders thou perforce must bear,
When they in thee the like offenses prove:
If but for fear of this, thy will remove;
    For princes are the glass, the school, the book,
    Where subjects' eyes do learn, do read, do look.

"And wilt thou be the school when Lust shall learn?
Must he in thee read lectures of such shame?
Wilt thou be glass wherein it shall discern
Authority for sin, warrant for blame?
To privilege dishonor in thy name,
    Thou back'st reproach against long-living laud,
    And mak'st fair reputation but a bawd.

"Hast thou command? By him that gave it thee,
From a pure heart command thy rebel will:
Draw not thy sword to guard iniquity,
For it was lent thee all that brood to kill.
Thy princely office how canst thou fulfill,
    When, patterned by thy fault, foul Sin may say,
    He learn'd to sin, and thou didst teach the way?

"Think but how vile a spectacle it were,
To view thy present trespass in another.
Men's faults do seldom to themselves appear;
Their own transgressions partially they smother:

This guilt would seem death-worthy in thy brother.
O, how are they wrapped in with infamies,
That from their own misdeeds askance their eyes!

"To thee, to thee, my heaved-up hands appeal,
Not to seducing lust, thy rash relier;
I sue for exiled majesty's repeal;
Let him return, and flatt'ring thoughts retire:
His true respect will prison false desire,
    And wipe the dim mist from thy doting eyne,
    That thou shalt see thy state, and pity mine."

"Have done," quoth he; "my uncontrollèd tide
Turns not, but swells the higher by this let.
Small lights are soon blown out, huge fires abide,
And with the wind in greater fury fret:
The petty streams that pay a daily debt
    To their salt sovereign, with their fresh falls' haste,
    Add to his flow, but alter not his taste."

"Thou art," quoth she, "a sea, a sovereign king;
And lo, there falls into thy boundless flood
Black lust, dishonor, shame, misgoverning,
Who seek to stain the ocean of thy blood.
If all these petty ills shall change thy good,
    Thy sea within a puddle's womb is hearsed,
    And not the puddle in thy sea dispersed.

"So shall these slaves be king, and thou their slave;
Thou nobly base, they basely dignified;
Thou their fair life, and they thy fouler grave;
Thou loathèd in their shame, they in thy pride:
The lesser thing should not the greater hide;
    The cedar stoops not to the base shrub's foot,
    But low shrubs wither at the cedar's root.

"So let thy thoughts, low vassals to thy state"—
"No more," quoth he, "by heaven, I will not hear thee!
Yield to my love; if not, enforcèd hate,
Instead of love's coy touch, shall rudely tear thee;
That done, despitefully I mean to bear thee
    Unto the base bed of some rascal groom,
    To be thy partner in this shameful doom."

This said, he sets his foot upon the light,
For light and lust are deadly enemies:
Shame folded up in blind-concealing night,
When most unseen, then most doth tyrannize.
The wolf hath seized his prey, the poor lamb cries;
    Till with her own white fleece her voice controlled
    Entombs her outcry in her lips' sweet fold:

For with the nightly linen that she wears
He pens her piteous clamors in her head;
Cooling his hot face in the chastest tears
That ever modest eyes with sorrow shed.
O, that prone lust should stain so pure a bed!
    The spots whereof could weeping purify,
    Her tears should drop on them perpetually.

But she hath lost a dearer thing than life,
And he hath won what he would lose again:
This forcèd league doth force a further strife;
This momentary joy breeds months of pain;
This hot desire converts to cold disdain:
    Pure Chastity is rifled of her store,
    And Lust, the thief, far poorer than before.

Look, as the full-fed hound or gorgèd hawk,
Unapt for tender smell or speedy flight,
Make slow pursuit, or altogether balk

The prey wherein by nature they delight;
So surfeit-taking Tarquin fares this night:
His taste delicious, in digestion souring,
Devours his will, that lived by foul devouring.

O, deeper sin than bottomless conceit
Can comprehend in still imagination!
Drunken Desire must vomit his receipt,
Ere he can see his own abomination.
While Lust is in his pride, no exclamation
Can curb his head, or rein his rash desire,
Till, like a jade, self-will himself doth tire.

And then with lank and lean discolored cheek,
With heavy eye, knit brow, and strengthless pace,
Feeble Desire, all recreant, poor, and meek,
Like to a bankrupt beggar wails his case:
The flesh being proud, Desire doth fight with Grace,
For there it revels; and when that decays,
The guilty rebel for remission prays.

So fares it with this faultful lord of Rome,
Who this accomplishment so hotly chased;
For now against himself he sounds this doom—
That through the length of time he stands disgraced:
Besides, his soul's fair temple is defaced;
To whose weak ruins muster troops of cares,
To ask the spotted princess how she fares.

She says, her subjects with foul insurrection
Have battered down her consecrated wall,
And by their mortal fault brought in subjection
Her immortality, and made her thrall
To living death and pain perpetual:

Which in her prescience she controllèd still,
But her foresight could not forestall their will.

Even in this thought through the dark night he
     stealeth,
A captive victor that hath lost in gain;
Bearing away the wound that nothing healeth,
The scar that will, despite of cure, remain;
Leaving his spoil perplexed in greater pain.
     She bears the load of lust he left behind,
     And he the burden of a guilty mind.

He like a thievish dog creeps sadly thence;
She like a wearied lamb lies panting there;
He scowls, and hates himself for his offense;
She, desperate, with her nails her flesh doth tear;
He faintly flies, sweating with guilty fear;
     She stays, exclaiming on the direful night;
     He runs, and chides his vanished, loathed delight.

He thence departs a heavy convertite;
She there remains a hopeless castaway;
He in his speed looks for the morning light;
She prays she never may behold the day;
"For day," quoth she, "night's scapes doth open lay,
     And my true eyes have never practiced how
     To cloak offenses with a cunning brow.

"They think not but that every eye can see
The same disgrace which they themselves behold;
And therefore would they still in darkness be,
To have their unseen sin remain untold;
For they their guilt with weeping will unfold,
     And grave, like water, that doth eat in steel,
     Upon my cheeks what helpless shame I feel."

Here she exclaims against repose and rest,
And bids her eyes hereafter still be blind.
She wakes her heart by beating on her breast,
And bids it leap from thence, where it may find
Some purer chest to close so pure a mind.
    Frantic with grief, thus breathes she forth her spite
    Against the unseen secrecy of night:

"O comfort-killing Night, image of hell!
Dim register and notary of shame!
Black stage for tragedies and murders fell!
Vast sin-concealing chaos! nurse of blame!
Blind muffled bawd! Dark harbor for defame!
    Grim cave of death! Whispering conspirator
    With close-tongued treason and the ravisher!

"O, hateful, vaporous, and foggy Night!
Since thou art guilty of my cureless crime,
Muster thy mists to meet the eastern light,
Make war against proportioned course of time;
Or if thou wilt permit the sun to climb
    His wonted height, yet ere he go to bed,
    Knit poisonous clouds about his golden head.

"With rotten damps ravish the morning air;
Let their exhaled unwholesome breaths make sick
The life of purity, the supreme fair,
Ere he arrive his weary noontide prick;
And let thy misty vapors march so thick,
    That in their smoky ranks his smothered light
    May set at noon, and make perpetual night.

"Were Tarquin Night (as he is but Night's child),
The silver-shining queen he would distain;

Her twinkling handmaids too, by him defiled,
Through Night's black bosom should not peep again:
So should I have co-partners in my pain;
    And fellowship in woe doth woe assuage,
    As palmers' chat makes short their pilgrimage.

"Where now I have no one to blush with me,
To cross their arms, and hang their heads with mine,
To mark their brows, and hide their infamy;
But I alone must sit and pine,
Seasoning the earth with showers of silver brine,
    Mingling my talk with tears, my grief with groans,
    Poor wasting monuments of lasting moans.

"O Night, thou furnace of foul reeking smoke,
Let not the jealous Day behold that face
Which underneath thy black all-hiding cloak
Immodestly lies martyred with disgrace!
Keep still possession of thy gloomy place,
    That all the faults which in thy reign are made
    May likewise be sepulchred in thy shade!

"Make me not object to the tell-tale Day!
The light will show, charactered in my brow,
The story of sweet chastity's decay,
The impious breach of holy wedlock vow:
Yea, the illiterate, that know not how
    To cipher what is writ in learnèd books,
    Will quote my loathsome trespass in my looks.

"The nurse, to still her child, will tell my story,
And fright her crying babe with Tarquin's name;
The orator, to deck his oratory,
Will couple my reproach to Tarquin's shame;

Feast-finding minstrels, tuning my defame,
Will tie the hearers to attend each line,
How Tarquin wrongèd me, I Collatine.

"Let my good name, that senseless reputation,
For Collatine's dear love be kept unspotted:
If that be made a theme for disputation,
The branches of another root are rotted,
And undeserved reproach to him allotted
    That is as clear from this attaint of mine,
    As I, ere this, was pure to Collatine.

"O unseen shame, invisible disgrace!
O unfelt sore, crest-wounding, private scar!
Reproach is stamped in Collatinus' face,
And Tarquin's eye may read the mot afar,
How he in peace is wounded, not in war.
    Alas, how many bear such shameful blows,
    Which not themselves, but he that gives them
        knows!

"If, Collatine, thine honor lay in me,
From me by strong assault it is bereft.
My honey lost, and I, a drone-like bee,
Have no perfection of my summer left,
But robbed and ransacked by injurious theft:
    In thy weak hive a wandering wasp hath crept,
    And sucked the honey which thy chaste bee kept.

"Yet am I guilty of thy honor's wrack—
Yet for thy honor did I entertain him;
Coming from thee, I could not push him back,
For it had been dishonor to disdain him:
Besides, of weariness he did complain him,
    And talked of virtue—O, unlooked-for evil,
    When virtue is profaned in such a devil!

"Why should the worm intrude the maiden bud?
Or hateful cuckoos hatch in sparrows' nests?
Or toads infect fair founts with venom mud?
Or tyrant folly lurk in gentle breasts?
Or kings be breakers of their own behests?
   But no perfection is so absolute,
   That some impurity doth not pollute.

"The aged man that coffers-up his gold
Is plagued with cramps, and gouts and painful fits;
And scarce hath eyes his treasure to behold,
But like still-pining Tantalus he sits,
And useless barns the harvest of his wits;
   Having no other pleasure of his gain
   But torment that it cannot cure his pain.

"So then he hath it, when he cannot use it,
And leaves it to be mastered by his young,
Who in their pride so presently abuse it:
Their father was too weak, and they too strong,
To hold their cursèd-blessèd fortune long.
   The sweets we wish for turn to loathèd sours,
   Even in the moment that we call them ours.

"Unruly blasts wait on the tender spring;
Unwholesome weeds take root with precious flowers;
The adder hisses where the sweet birds sing;
What virtue breeds iniquity devours:
We have no good that we can say is ours,
   But ill-annexèd Opportunity
   Or kills his life or else his quality.

"O Opportunity, thy guilt is great!
'Tis thou that execut'st the traitor's treason;
Thou sett'st the wolf where he the lamb may get;
Whoever plots the sin, thou point'st the season;

'Tis thou that spurn'st at right, at law, at reason;
And in thy shady cell, where none may spy him,
Sits Sin, to seize the souls that wander by him.

"Thou mak'st the vestal violate her oath;
Thou blow'st the fire when temperance is thawed;
Thou smother'st honesty, thou murder'st troth;
Thou foul abettor, thou notorious bawd!
Thou plantest scandal, and displacest laud:
Thou ravisher, thou traitor, thou false thief,
Thy honey turns to gall, thy joy to grief!

"Thy secret pleasure turns to open shame,
Thy private feasting to a public fast,
Thy smoothing titles to a ragged name;
Thy sugared tongue to bitter wormwood taste:
Thy violent vanities can never last.
How comes it, then, vile Opportunity,
Being so bad, such numbers seek for thee?

"When wilt thou be the humble suppliant's friend,
And bring him where his suit may be obtained?
When wilt thou sort an hour great strifes to end?
Or free that soul which wretchedness hath chained?
Give physic to the sick, ease to the pained
The poor, lame, blind, halt, creep, cry out for
thee;
But they ne'er meet with Opportunity.

"The patient dies while the physician sleeps;
The orphan pines while the oppressor feeds;
Justice is feasting while the widow weeps;
Advice is sporting while infection breeds;
Thou grant'st no time for charitable deeds;

Wrath, envy, treason, rape, and murder's rages,
Thy heinous hours wait on them as their pages.

"When Truth and Virtue have to do with thee
A thousand crosses keep them from thy aid:
They buy the help; but Sin ne'er gives a fee,
He gratis comes; and thou art well appaid
As well to hear as grant what he hath said.
    My Collatine would else have come to me
    When Tarquin did, but he was stayed by thee.

"Guilty thou art of murder and of theft;
Guilty of perjury and subornation;
Guilty of treason, forgery, and shift;
Guilty of incest, that abomination:
An accessary by thine inclination
    To all sins past, and all that are to come,
    From the creation to the general doom.

"Misshapen Time, copesmate of ugly Night,
Swift-subtle post, carrier of grisly care,
Eater of youth, false slave to false delight,
Base watch of woes, sin's pack horse, virtue's snare;
Thou nursest all, and murder'st all that are:
    O, hear me, then, injurious-shifting Time!
    Be guilty of my death, since of my crime.

"Why hath thy servant, Opportunity,
Betrayed the hours thou gav'st me to repose?
Canceled my fortunes, and enchainèd me
To endless date of never-ending woes?
Time's office is to fine the hate of foes;
    To eat up errors by opinion bred,
    Not spend the dowry of a lawful bed.

"Time's glory is to calm contending kings,
To unmask falsehood, and bring truth to light,
To stamp the seal of time in agèd things,
To wake the morn, and sentinel the night,
To wrong the wronger till he render right,
  To ruinate proud buildings with thy hours,
  And smear with dust their glitt'ring golden towers;

"To fill with wormholes stately monuments,
To feed oblivion with decay of things,
To blot old books and alter their contents,
To pluck the quills from ancient ravens' wings,
To dry the old oak's sap, and cherish springs,
  To spoil antiquities of hammered steel,
  And turn the giddy round of Fortune's wheel;

"To show the beldame daughters of her daughter,
To make the child a man, the man a child,
To slay the tiger that doth live by slaughter,
To tame the unicorn and lion wild,
To mock the subtle in themselves beguiled;
  To cheer the ploughman with increaseful crops,
  And waste huge stones with little water drops.

"Why work'st thou mischief in thy pilgrimage,
Unless thou couldst return to make amends?
One poor retiring minute in an age
Would purchase thee a thousand-thousand friends,
Lending him wit that to bad debtors lends:
  O, this dread night, wouldst thou one hour come back,
  I could prevent this storm, and shun thy wrack!

"Thou ceaseless lackey to eternity,
With some mischance cross Tarquin in his flight:

Devise extremes beyond extremity,
To make him curse this cursèd crimeful night:
Let ghastly shadows his lewd eyes affright;
  And the dire thought of his committed evil
  Shape every bush a hideous-shapeless devil.

"Disturb his hours of rest with restless trances,
Afflict him in his bed with bedrid groans;
Let there bechance him pitiful mischances,
To make him moan, but pity not his moans·
Stone him with hardened hearts, harder than stones;
  And let mild women to him lose their mildness,
  Wilder to him than tigers in their wildness.

"Let him have time to tear his curlèd hair,
Let him have time against himself to rave,
Let him have time of Time's help to despair,
Let him have time to live a loathèd slave,
Let him have time a beggar's orts to crave;
  And time to see one that by alms doth live
  Disdain to him disdainèd scraps to give.

"Let him have time to see his friends his foes,
And merry fools to mock at him resort;
Let him have time to mark how slow time goes
In time of sorrow, and how swift and short
His time of folly and his time of sport;
  And ever let his unrecalling crime
  Have time to wail th'abusing of his time.

"O Time, thou tutor both to good and bad,
Teach me to curse him that thou taught'st this ill!
At his own shadow let the thief run mad,
Himself himself seek every hour to kill!

Such wretched hands such wretched blood should spill;
    For who so base would such an office have
    As sland'rous deathsman to so base a slave?

"The baser is he, coming from a king,
To shame his hope with deeds degenerate:
The mightier man, the mightier is the thing
That makes him honored, or begets him hate;
For greatest scandal waits on greatest state.
    The moon being clouded presently is missed,
    But little stars may hide them when they list.

"The crow may bathe his coal-black wings in mire,
And unperceived fly with the filth away;
But if the like the snow-white swan desire,
The stain upon his silver down will stay.
Poor grooms are sightless night, kings glorious day.
    Gnats are unnoted wheresoe'er they fly,
    But eagles gaz'd upon with every eye.

"Out, idle words, servants to shallow fools!
Unprofitable sounds, weak arbitrators!
Busy yourselves in skill-contending schools,
Debate where leisure serves with dull debaters;
To trembling clients be you mediators:
    For me, I force not argument a straw,
    Since that my case is past the help of law.

"In vain I rail at Opportunity,
At Time, at Tarquin, and uncheerful Night;
In vain I cavil with my infamy,
In vain I spurn at my confirmed despite:
This helpless smoke of words doth me no right.
    This remedy indeed to do me good,
    Is to let forth my foul-defilèd blood.

"Poor hand, why quiver'st thou at this decree?
Honor thyself to rid me of this shame;
For if I die, my honor lives in thee;
But if I live, thou liv'st in my defame:
Since thou couldst not defend thy loyal dame,
  And wast afeared to scratch her wicked foe,
  Kill both thyself and her for yielding so."

This said, from her betumbled couch she starteth,
To find some desperate instrument of death:
But this no slaughterhouse no tool imparteth,
To make more vent for passage of her breath,
Which, thronging through her lips, so vanisheth
  As smoke from Aetna, that in air consumes,
  Or that which from dischargèd cannon fumes.

"In vain," quoth she, "I live, and seek in vain
Some happy mean to end a hapless life.
I feared by Tarquin's falchion to be slain,
Yet for the selfsame purpose seek a knife:
But when I feared I was a loyal wife:
  So am I now—O no, that cannot be;
  Of that true type hath Tarquin rifled me!

"O, that is gone for which I sought to live,
And therefore now I need not fear to die.
To clear this spot by death, at least I give
A badge of fame to slander's livery;
A dying life to living infamy:
  Poor helpless help, the treasure stol'n away,
  To burn the guiltless casket where it lay!

"Well, well, dear Collatine, thou shalt not know
The stainèd taste of violated troth;
I will not wrong thy true affection so,

To flatter thee with an infringèd oath;
This bastard graft shall never come to growth:
    He shall not boast who did thy stock pollute
    That thou art doting father of his fruit.

"Nor shall he smile at thee in secret thought,
Nor laugh with his companions at thy state;
But thou shalt know thy int'rest was not bought
Basely with gold, but stol'n from forth thy gate.
For me, I am the mistress of my fate,
    And with my trespass never will dispense,
    Till life to death acquit my forced offense.

"I will not poison thee with my attaint,
Nor fold my fault in cleanly-coined excuses;
My sable ground of sin I will not paint,
To hide the truth of this false night's abuses:
My tongue shall utter all; mine eyes like sluices,
    As from a mountain spring that feeds a dale,
    Shall gush pure streams to purge my impure tale."

By this, lamenting Philomel had ended
The well-tuned warble of her nightly sorrow,
And solemn night with slow-sad gait descended
To ugly hell; when, lo the blushing morrow
Lends light to all fair eyes that light will borrow;
    But cloudy Lucrece shames herself to see,
    And therefore still in night would cloistered be.

Revealing day through every cranny spies,
And seems to point her out where she sits weeping;
To whom she sobbing speaks: "O, eye of eyes,
Why pryest thou through my window? Leave thy peeping;
Mock with thy tickling beams eyes that are sleeping;

Brand not my forehead with thy piercing light,
For day hath nought to do what's done by night."

Thus cavils she with everything she sees:
True grief is fond and testy as a child,
Who wayward once, his mood with nought agrees.
Old woes, not infant sorrows, bear them mild;
Continuance tames the one; the other wild,
    Like an unpracticed swimmer plunging still,
    With too much labor drowns for want of skill.

So she, deep drenchèd in a sea of care,
Holds disputation with each thing she views,
And to herself all sorrow doth compare;
No object but her passion's strength renews;
And as one shifts, another straight ensues:
    Sometime her grief is dumb, and hath no words;
    Sometime 'tis mad, and too much talk affords.

The little birds that tune their morning's joy
Make her moans mad with their sweet melody:
For mirth doth search the bottom of annoy;
Sad souls are slain in merry company;
Grief best is pleased with grief's society:
    True sorrow then is feelingly sufficed
    When with like semblance it is sympathized.

'Tis double death to drown in ken of shore;
He ten times pines that pines beholding food;
To see the salve doth make the wound ache more;
Great grief grieves most at that would do it good;
Deep woes roll forward like a gentle flood,
    Who, being stopped, the hounding banks o'erflows;
    Grief dallied with nor law nor limit knows.

"You mocking birds," quoth she, "your tunes entomb
Within your hollow-swelling feathered breasts,
And in my hearing be you mute and dumb!
My restless discord loves no stops nor rests;
A woeful hostess brooks not merry guests:
    Relish your nimble notes to pleasing ears;
    Distress likes dumps when time is kept with tears.

"Come, Philomel, that sing'st of ravishment,
Make thy sad grove in my disheveled hair:
As the dank earth weeps at thy languishment,
So I at each sad strain will strain a tear,
And with deep groans the diapason bear;
    For burden-wise I'll hum on Tarquin still,
    While thou on Tereus descant'st better still.

"And whiles against a thorn thou bear'st thy part,
To keep thy sharp woes waking, wretched I,
To imitate thee well, against my heart
Will fix a sharp knife, to affright mine eye;
Who, if it wink, shall thereon fall and die.
    These means, as frets upon an instrument,
    Shall tune our heartstrings to true languishment.

"And for, poor bird, thou sing'st not in the day,
As shaming any eye should thee behold,
Some dark-deep desert, seated from the way,
That knows not parching heat nor freezing cold,
We will find out; and there we will unfold
    To creatures stern sad tunes, to change their kinds:
    Since men prove beasts let beasts bear gentle minds."

As the poor frightened deer, that stands at gaze,
Wildly determining which way to fly,

Or one encompassed with a winding maze,
That cannot tread the way out readily;
So with herself is she in mutiny,
    To live or die which of the twain were better.
    When life is shamed, and death reproach's debtor.

"To kill myself," quoth she, "alack! what were it,
But with my body my poor soul's pollution?
They that lose half with greater patience bear it
Than they whose whole is swallowed in confusion.
That mother tries a merciless conclusion
    Who, having two sweet babes, when death takes one,
    Will slay the other, and be nurse to none.

"My body or my soul, which was the dearer,
When the one pure, the other made divine?
Whose love of either to myself was nearer,
When both were kept for heaven and Collatine?
Ay me! the bark peeled from the lofty pine,
    His leaves will wither, and his sap decay;
    So must my soul, her bark being peeled away.

"Her house is sacked, her quiet interrupted,
Her mansion battered by the enemy;
Her sacred temple spotted, spoiled, corrupted,
Grossly engirt with daring infamy:
Then let it not be called impiety,
    If in this blemished fort I make some hole
    Through which I may convey this troubled soul.

"Yet die I will not till my Collatine
Have heard the cause of my untimely death;
That he may vow, in that sad hour of mine,
Revenge on him that made me stop my breath.

My stainèd blood to Tarquin I'll bequeath,
Which by him tainted shall for him be spent,
And as his due, writ in my testament.

"My honor I'll bequeath unto the knife
That wounds my body so dishonorèd.
'Tis honor to deprive dishonored life;
The one will live, the other being dead:
So of shame's ashes shall my fame be bred;
For in my death I murder shameful scorn:
My shame so dead, mine honor is newborn.

"Dear lord of that dear jewel I have lost,
What legacy shall I bequeath to thee?
My resolution, love, shall be thy boast,
By whose example thou revenged mayst be.
How Tarquin must be used, read it in me:
Myself, thy friend, will kill myself, thy foe,
And, for my sake, serve thou false Tarquin so.

"This brief abridgment of my will I make—
My soul and body to the skies and ground;
My resolution, husband, do thou take;
Mine honor be the knife's that makes my wound;
My shame be his that did my fame confound;
And all my fame that lives disbursèd be
To those that live, and think no shame of me.

"Thou, Collatine, shalt oversee this will;
How I was overseen that thou shalt see it!
My blood shall wash the slander of mine ill;
My life's foul deed, my life's fair end shall free it.
Faint not, faint heart, but stoutly say, 'So be it.'
Yield to my hand; my hand shall conquer thee:
Thou dead, both die, and both shall victors be."

This plot of death when sadly she had laid,
And wiped the brinish pearl from her bright eyes,
With untuned tongue she hoarsely called her maid,
Whose swift obedience to her mistress hies;
For fleet-winged duty with thought's feathers flies.
   Poor Lucrece' cheeks unto her maid seem so
   As winter meads when sun doth melt their snow.

Her mistress she doth give demure good-morrow,
With soft-slow tongue, true mark of modesty,
And sorts a sad look to her lady's sorrow,
For why her face wore sorrow's livery;
But durst not ask of her audaciously
   Why her two suns were cloud-eclipsèd so,
   Now why her fair cheeks over-washed with woe.

But as the earth doth weep, the sun being set,
Each flower moistened like a melting eye;
Even so the maid with swelling drops 'gan wet
Her circled eyne, enforced by sympathy
Of those fair suns set in her mistress' sky,
   Who in a salt-waved ocean quenched their light,
   Which makes the maid weep like the dewy night.

A pretty while these pretty creatures stand,
Like ivory conduits coral cisterns filling:
One justly weeps; the other takes in hand
No cause, but company, of her drops spilling:
Their gentle sex to weep are often willing;
   Grieving themselves to guess at others' smarts,
   And then they drown their eyes, or break their hearts.

For men have marble, women waxen minds,
And therefore are they formed as marble will;
The weak oppressed, th'impression of strange kinds

Is formed in them by force, by fraud, or skill:
Then call them not the authors of their ill,
  No more than wax shall be accounted evil,
  Wherein is stamped the semblance of a devil.

. Their smoothness, like a goodly champaign plain,
Lays open all the little worms that creep;
In men, as in a rough-grown grove, remain
Cave-keeping evils that obscurely sleep:
Through crystal walls each little mote will peep:
  Though men can cover crimes with bold stern looks,
  Poor women's faces are their own faults' books.

No man inveigh against the withered flower,
But chide rough winter that the flower hath killed:
Not that devoured, but that which doth devour,
Is worthy blame. O, let it not be hild
Poor women's faults that they are so fulfilled
  With men's abuses, those proud lords, to blame,
  Make weak-made women tenants to their shame.

The precedent whereof in Lucrece' view,
Assailed by night with circumstances strong
Of present death, and shame that might ensue
By that her death, to do her husband wrong:
Such danger to resistance did belong,
  That dying fear through all her body spread;
  And who cannot abuse a body dead?

By this, mild patience bid fair Lucrece speak
To the poor counterfeit of her complaining:
"My girl," quoth she, "on what occasion break
Those tears from thee, that down thy cheeks are raining?
If thou dost weep for grief of my sustaining,

Know, gentle wench, it small avails my mood:
If tears could help, mine own would do me good.

"But tell me, girl, when went"—and there she stayed
Till after a deep groan—"Tarquin from hence?"
"Madam, ere I was up," replied the maid,
"The more to blame my sluggard negligence:
Yet with the fault I thus far can dispense—
    Myself was stirring ere the break of day,
    And, ere I rose, was Tarquin gone away.

"But lady, if your maid may be so bold,
She would request to know your heaviness."
"O, peace," quoth Lucrece; "if it should be told,
The repetition cannot make it less;
For more it is than I can well express:
    And that deep torture may be called a hell,
    When more is felt than one hath power to tell.

"Go, get me hither paper, ink, and pen—
Yet save that labor, for I have them here.
What should I say? One of my husband's men
Bid thou be ready, by and by, to bear
A letter to my lord, my love, my dear:
    Bid him with speed prepare to carry it;
    The cause craves haste, and it will soon be writ."

Her maid is gone, and she prepares to write,
First hovering o'er the paper with her quill:
Conceit and grief an eager combat fight;
What wit sets down is blotted straight with will;
This is too curious-good, this blunt and ill:
    Much like a press of people at a door,
    Throng her inventions, which shall go before.

At last she thus begins—"Thou worthy lord
Of that unworthy wife that greeteth thee,
Health to thy person! Next vouchsafe t'afford
(If ever, love, thy Lucrece thou wilt see)
Some present speed to come and visit me.
   So I commend me from our house in grief:
   My woes are tedious, though my words are brief."

Here she folds up the tenor of her woe,
Her certain sorrow writ uncertainly.
By this short schedule Collatine may know
Her grief, but not her grief's true quality;
She dares not thereof make discovery,
   Lest he should hold it her own gross abuse,
   Ere she with blood had stained her stain's excuse.

Besides, the life and feeling of her passion
She hoards, to spend when he is by to hear her;
When sighs and groans and tears may grace the fashion
Of her disgrace, the better so to clear her
From that suspicion which the world might bear her.
   To shun this blot, she would not blot the letter
   With words, till action might become them better.

To see sad sights moves more than hear them told;
For then the eye interprets to the ear
The heavy motion that it doth behold:
When every part a part of woe doth bear,
'Tis but a part of sorrow that we hear:
   Deep sounds make lesser noise than shallow fords,
   And sorrow ebbs, being blown with wind of words.

Her letter now is sealed, and on it writ,
"At Ardea to my lord with more than haste."

The post attends, and she delivers it,
Charging the sour-faced groom to hie as fast
As lagging fowls before the northern blast:
    Speed more than speed but dull and slow she deems:
    Extremity still urgeth such extremes.

The homely villain curtsies to her low;
And, blushing on her, with a steadfast eye
Receives the scroll without or yea or no,
And forth with bashful innocence doth hie.
But they whose guilt within their bosoms lie
    Imagine every eye beholds their blame;
    For Lucrece thought he blushed to see her shame:

When, silly groom, God wot, it was defect
Of spirit, life, and bold audacity.
Such harmless creatures have a true respect
To talk in deeds, while others saucily
Promise more speed, but do it leisurely:
    Even so this pattern of the worn-out age
    Pawned honest looks, but laid no words to gage.

His kindled duty kindled her mistrust
That two red fires in both their faces blazed;
She thought he blushed, as knowing Tarquin's lust,
And, blushing with him, wistly on him gazed;
Her earnest eye did make him more amazed:
    The more she saw the blood his cheeks replenish,
    The more she thought he spied in her some blemish.

But long she thinks till he return again,
And yet the duteous vassal scarce is gone.
The weary time she cannot entertain,
For now 'tis stale to sigh, to weep, and groan:

So woe hath wearied woe, moan tired moan,
  That she plaints a little while doth stay,
  Pausing for means to mourn some newer way.

At last she calls to mind where hangs a piece
Of skillful painting, made for Priam's Troy;
Before the which is drawn the power of Greece,
For Helen's rape the city to destroy,
Threat'ning cloud-kissing Ilion with annoy;
  Which the conceited painter drew so proud,
  As heaven, it seemed, to kiss the turrets bowed.

A thousand lamentable objects there,
In scorn of nature, art gave lifeless life:
Many a dry drop seemed a weeping tear,
Shed for the slaughtered husband by the wife:
The red blood reeked to show the painter's strife;
  And dying eyes gleamed forth their ashy lights,
  Like dying coals burnt out in tedious nights.

There might you see the laboring pioneer
Begrimed with sweat, and smearèd all with dust;
And from the towers of Troy there would appear
The very eyes of men through loopholes thrust,
Gazing upon the Greeks with little lust:
  Such a sweet observance in this work was had,
  That one might see those far-off eyes look sad.

In great commanders grace and majesty
You might behold, triumphing in their faces;
In youth, quick bearing and dexterity;
And here and there the painter interlaces
Pale cowards, marching on with trembling paces
  Which heartless peasants did so well resemble,
  That one would swear he saw them quake and tremble.

In Ajax and Ulysses, O, what art
Of physiognomy might one behold!
The face of either ciphered either's heart;
Their face their manners most expressly told:
In Ajax' eyes blunt rage and rigor rolled;
    But the mild glance that sly Ulysses lent,
    Showed deep regard and smiling government.

There pleading might you see grave Nestor stand,
As 'twere encouraging the Greeks to fight;
Making such sober action with his hand
That it beguiled attention, charmed the sight:
In speech, it seemed, his beard all silver white
    Wagged up and down, and from his lips did fly
    Thin winding breath, which purled up to the sky.

About him were a press of gaping faces,
Which seemed to swallow up his sound advice;
All jointly listening, but with several graces,
As if some mermaid did their ears entice;
Some high, some low; the painter was so nice,
    The scalps of many, almost hid behind,
    To jump up higher seemed, to mock the mind.

Here one man's hand leaned on another's head,
His nose being shadowed by his neighbor's ear;
Here one, being thronged, bears back, all boll'n and red;
Another, smothered, seems to pelt and swear;
And in their rage such signs of rage they bear,
    As, but for loss of Nestor's golden words,
    It seemed they would debate with angry swords.

For much imaginary work was there;
Conceit deceitful, so compact, so kind,
That for Achilles' image stood his spear,

Gripped in an armèd hand; himself, behind,
Was left unseen, save to the eye of mind:
   A hand, a foot, a face, a leg, a head,
   Stood for the whole to be imaginèd.

And from the walls of strong-besiegèd Troy
When their brave hope, bold Hector, marched to field,
Stood many Trojan mothers, sharing joy
To see their youthful sons bright weapons wield;
And to their hope they such odd action yield,
   That through their light joy seemèd to appear
   Like bright things stained, a kind of heavy fear.

And from the strand of Dardan, where they fought,
To Simois' reedy banks the red blood ran,
Whose waves to imitate the battle sought
With swelling ridges; and their ranks began
To break upon the gallèd shore, and than
   Retire again, till, meeting greater ranks,
   They join, and shoot their foam at Simois' banks.

To this well-painted piece is Lucrece come,
To find a face where all distress is stelled.
Many she sees where cares have carvèd some,
But none where all distress and dolor dwelled,
Till she despairing Hecuba beheld,
   Staring on Priam's wounds with her old eyes,
   Which bleeding under Pyrrhus' proud foot lies.

In her the painter had anatomized
Time's ruin, beauty's wreck, and grim care's reign:
Her cheeks with chaps and wrinkles were disguised;
Of what she was no semblance did remain:
Her blue blood changed to black in every vein,

Wanting the spring that those shrunk pipes had fed,
Showed life imprisoned in a body dead.

On this sad shadow Lucrece spends her eyes,
And shapes her sorrow to the beldame's woes,
Who nothing wants to answer her but cries,
And bitter words to ban her cruel foes:
The painter was no god to lend her those;
    And therefore Lucrece swears he did her wrong,
    To give her so much grief, and not a tongue.

"Poor instrument," quoth she, "without a sound,
I'll tune thy woes with my lamenting tongue;
And drop sweet balm in Priam's painted wound,
And rail on Pyrrhus that hath done him wrong;
And with my tears quench Troy that burns so long;
    And with my knife scratch out the angry eyes
    Of all the Greeks that are thine enemies.

"Show me the strumpet that began this stir,
That with my nails her beauty I may tear.
Thy heat of lust, fond Paris, did incur
This load of wrath that burning Troy doth bear:
Thine eye kindled the fire that burneth here;
    And here in Troy, for trespass of thine eye,
    The sire, the son, the dame, and daughter die.

"Why should the private pleasure of someone
Become the public plague of many moe?
Let sin, alone committed, light alone
Upon his head that hath transgressèd so;
Let guiltless souls be freed from guilty woe:
    For one's offense why should so many fall,
    To plague a private sin in general?

"Lo, here weeps Hecuba, here Priam dies,
Here manly Hector faints, here Troilus swounds,
Here friend by friend in bloody channel lies,
And friend to friend gives unadvisèd wounds,
And one man's lust these many lives confounds:
    Had doting Priam checked his son's desire,
    Troy had been bright with fame, and not with fire."

Here feelingly she weeps Troy's painted woes:
For sorrow, like a heavy-hanging bell,
Once set on ringing, with his own weight goes;
Then little strength rings out the doleful knell:
So Lucrece, set a-work, sad tales doth tell
    To penciled pensiveness and colored sorrow;
    She lends them words, and she their looks doth borrow.

She throws her eyes about the painting round,
And whom she finds forlorn she doth lament.
At last she sees a wretched image bound,
That piteous looks to Phrygian shepherds lent;
His face, though full of cares, yet showed content.
    Onward to Troy with the blunt swains he goes,
    So mild, that Patience seemed to scorn his woes.

In him the painter labored with his skill
To hide deceit, and give the harmless show
A humble gait, calm looks, eyes wailing still,
A brow unbent, that seemed to welcome woe;
Cheeks neither red nor pale, but mingled so
    That blushing red no guilty instance gave,
    Nor ashy pale the fear that false hearts have.

But, like a constant and confirmèd devil,
He entertained a show so seeming just,

And therein so ensconced his secret evil,
That jealousy itself could not mistrust
False-creeping craft and perjury should thrust
    Into so bright a day such blackfaced storms,
    Or blot with hell-born sin such saint-like forms.

The well-skilled workman this mild image drew
For perjured Sinon, whose enchanting story
The credulous old Priam after slew;
Whose words, like wild-fire, burnt the shining glory
Of rich-built Ilion, that the skies were sorry,
    And little stars shot from their fixèd places,
    When their glass fell wherein they viewed their faces.

This picture she advisedly perused,
And chid the painter for his wondrous skill,
Saying, some shape in Sinon's was abused;
So fair a form lodged not a mind so ill:
And still on him she gazed, and gazing still,
    Such signs of truth in his plain face she spied,
    That she concludes the picture was belied.

"It cannot be," quoth she, "that so much guile"—
She would have said "can lurk in such a look";
But Tarquin's shape came in her mind the while,
And from her tongue "can lurk" from "cannot" took:
"It cannot be," she in that sense forsook,
    And turned it thus—"It cannot be, I find,
    But such a face should bear a wicked mind:

"For even as subtle Sinon here is painted,
So sober-sad, so weary, and so mild,
(As if with grief or travail he had fainted)
To me came Tarquin armèd; so beguiled

With outward honesty, but yet defiled
  With inward vice: as Priam did him cherish,
  So did I Tarquin; so my Troy did perish.

"Look, look, how list'ning Priam wets his eyes,
To see those borrowed tears that Sinon sheds!
Priam, why art thou old, and yet not wise?
For every tear he falls a Trojan bleeds:
His eye drops fire, no water thence proceeds;
  Those round clear pearls of his, that move thy pity,
  Are balls of quenchless fire to burn thy city.

"Such devils steal effects from lightless hell;
For Sinon in his fire doth quake with cold,
And in that cold hot-burning fire doth dwell;
These contraries such unity do hold,
Only to flatter fools, and make them bold:
  So Priam's trust false Sinon's tears doth flatter,
  That he finds means to burn his Troy with water."

Here, all enraged, such passion her assails,
That patience is quite beaten from her breast.
She tears the senseless Sinon with her nails,
Comparing him to that unhappy guest
Whose deed hath made herself herself detest:
  At last she smilingly with this gives o'er;
  "Fool! fool!" quoth she, "his wounds will not be sore."

Thus ebbs and flows the current of her sorrow,
And time doth weary time with her complaining.
She looks for night, and then she longs for morrow,
And both she thinks too long with her remaining:
Short time seems long in sorrow's sharp sustaining:
  Though woe be heavy, yet it seldom sleeps;
  And they that watch see time how slow it creeps.

Which all this time hath overslipped her thought,
That she with painted images hath spent;
Being from the feeling of her own grief brought
By deep surmise of others' detriment;
Losing her woes in shows of discontent.
    It easeth some, though none it ever cured,
    To think their dolor others have endured.

But now the mindful messenger, come back,
Brings home his lord and other company;
Who finds his Lucrece clad in mourning black;
And round about her tear-distainèd eye
Blue circles streamed like rainbows in the sky:
    These water-galls in her dim element
    Foretell new storms to those already spent.

Which when her sad-beholding husband saw,
Amazedly in her sad face he stares:
Her eyes, though sod in tears, looked red and raw,
Her lively color killed with deadly cares.
He hath no power to ask her how she fares;
    But stood, like old acquaintance in a trance,
    Met far from home, wond'ring each other's chance.

At last he takes her by the bloodless hand,
And thus begins: "What uncouth ill event
Hath thee befall'n, that thou dost trembling stand?
Sweet love, what spite hath thy fair color spent?
Why art thou thus attired in discontent?
    Unmask, dear-dear, this moody heaviness,
    And tell thy grief, that we may give redress."

Three times with sighs she gives her sorrow fire,
Ere once she can discharge one word of woe:
At length addressed to answer his desire,

She modestly prepares to let them know
Her honor is taken prisoner by the foe;
  While Collatine and his consorted lords
  With sad attention long to hear her words.

And now this pale swan in her wat'ry nest
Begins the sad dirge of her certain ending:
"Few words," quoth she, "shall fit the trespass best,
Where no excuse can give the fault amending:
In me more woes than words are now depending;
  And my laments would be drawn out too long,
  To tell them all with one poor tired tongue.

"Then be this all the task it hath to say:
Dear husband, in the interest of thy bed
A stranger came, and on that pillow lay
Where thou wast wont to rest thy weary head;
And what wrong else may be imaginèd
  By foul enforcement might be done to me,
  From that, alas, thy Lucrece is not free.

"For in the dreadful dead of dark midnight,
With shining falchion in my chamber came
A creeping creature, with a flaming light,
And softly cried, 'Awake, thou Roman dame,
And entertain my love; else lasting shame
  On thee and thine this night I will inflict,
  If thou my love's desire do contradict.

" 'For some hard-favored groom of thine,' quoth he,
'Unless thou yoke thy liking to my will,
I'll murder straight, and then I'll slaughter thee,
And swear I found you where you did fulfill
The loathsome act of lust, and so did kill

The lechers in their deed. This act will be
My fame, and thy perpetual infamy.'

"With this, I did begin to start and cry;
And then against my heart he set his sword,
Swearing, unless I took all patiently,
I should not live to speak another word;
So should my shame still rest upon record,
    And never be forgot in mighty Rome
    Th'adulterate death of Lucrece and her groom.

"Mine enemy was strong, my poor self weak,
And far the weaker with so strong a fear:
My bloody judge forbade my tongue to speak;
No rightful plea might plead for justice there:
His scarlet lust came evidence to swear
    That my poor beauty had purloined his eyes;
    And when the judge is robbed, the prisoner dies.

"O, teach me how to make mine own excuse!
Or, at the least, this refuge let me find—
Though my gross blood be stained with this abuse,
Immaculate and spotless in my mind;
That was not forced; that never was inclined
    To accessory yieldings, but still pure
    Doth in her poisoned closet yet endure."

Lo, here, the hopeless merchant of this loss,
With head declined, and voice damned up with woe,
With sad-set eyes, and wreathèd arms across,
From lips new-waxen pale begins to blow
The grief away that stops his answer so:
    But, wretched as he is, he strives in vain;
    What he breathes out his breath drinks up again.

As through an arch the violent-roaring tide
Outruns the eye that doth behold his haste,
Yet in the eddy boundeth in his pride
Back to the strait that forced him on so fast;
In rage sent out, recalled in rage, being past:
    Even so his sighs, his sorrows, make a saw,
      To push grief on, and back the same grief draw.

Which speechless woe of his poor she attendeth,
And his untimely frenzy thus awaketh:
"Dear lord, thy sorrow to my sorrow lendeth
Another power; no flood by raining slaketh.
My woe too sensible thy passion maketh
    More feeling-painful. Let it, then, suffice
      To drown one woe, one pair of weeping eyes.

"And for my sake, when I might charm thee so,
For she that was my Lucrece—not attend me:
Be suddenly revengèd upon my foe,
Thine, mine, his own: suppose thou dost defend me
From what is past; the help that thou shalt lend me
    Comes all too late, yet let the traitor die;
      For sparing justice feeds iniquity.

"But ere I name him, you, fair lords," quoth she,
Speaking to those that came with Collatine,
"Shall plight your honorable faiths to me,
With swift pursuit to venge this wrong of mine;
For 'tis a meritorious fair design
    To chase injustice with revengeful arms:
      Knights, by their oaths, should right poor ladies'
        harms."

At this request, with noble disposition
Each present lord began to promise aid,

As bound in knighthood to her imposition,
Longing to hear the hateful foe bewrayed:
But she, that yet her sad task hath not said,
 The protestation stops. "O, speak," quoth she,
 "How may this forcèd stain be wiped from me?

"What is the quality of mine offense?
Being constrained with dreadful circumstance,
May my pure mind with the foul act dispense?
My low-declinèd honor to advance,
May any terms acquit me from this chance?
 The poisoned fountain clears itself again;
 And why not I from this compellèd stain?"

With this, they all at once began to say,
Her body's stain her mind untainted clears;
While with a joyless smile she turns away
The face, that map which deep impression bears
Of hard misfortune, carved in it with tears.
 "No, no," quoth she, "no dame, hereafter living,
 By my excuse shall claim excuse's giving."

Here with a sigh, as if her heart would break,
She throws forth Tarquin's name: "He! he!" she says,
But more than "he!" her poor tongue could not speak;
Till after many accents and delays,
Untimely breathing, sick and short assays,
 She utters this, "He, he, fair lords, 'tis he,
 That guides this hand to give this wound to me!"

Even here she sheathèd in her harmless breast
A harmful knife, that thence her soul unsheathed:
That blow did bail it from the deep unrest
Of that polluted prison where it breathed:
Her contrite sighs unto the clouds bequeathed

Her wingèd sprite, and through her wounds doth fly
Life's lasting date from canceled destiny.

Stone-still astonished with this deadly deed,
Stood Collatine and all his lordly crew;
Till Lucrece' father, that beholds her bleed,
Himself on her self-slaughtered body threw;
And from the purple fountain Brutus drew
    The murderous knife, and, as it left the place,
    Her blood, in poor revenge, held it in chase;

And bubbling from her breast, it doth divide
In two slow rivers, that the crimson blood
Circles her body in on every side,
Who, like a late-sacked island, vastly stood
Bare and unpeopled in this fearful flood.
    Some of her blood still pure and red remained,
    And some looked black, and that false Tarquin
        stained.

About the mourning and congealèd face
Of that black blood a wat'ry rigol goes,
Which seems to weep upon the tainted place:
And ever since, as pitying Lucrece' woes,
Corrupted blood some watery token shows;
    And blood untainted still doth red abide,
    Blushing at that which is so putrefied.

"Daughter, dear daughter," old Lucretius cries,
"That life was mine which thou hast here deprived.
If in the child the father's image lies,
Where shall I live now Lucrece is unlived?
Thou wast not to this end from me derived.
    If children pre-decease progenitors,
    We are their offspring, and they none of ours.

"Poor broken glass, I often did behold
In thy sweet semblance my old age new born;
But now that fair-fresh mirror, dim and old,
Shows me a bare-boned death by time outworn:
O, from thy cheeks my image thou hast torn,
  And shivered all the beauty of my glass,
  That I no more can see what once I was!

"O time, cease thou thy course, and last no longer,
If they surcease to be that should survive!
Shall rotten death make conquest of the stronger,
And leave the falt'ring feeble souls alive?
The old bees die, the young possess their hive:
  They live, sweet Lucrece, live again, and see
  Thy father die, and not thy father thee!"

By this, starts Collatine as from a dream,
And bids Lucretius give his sorrow place;
And then in key-cold Lucrece' bleeding stream
He falls, and bathes the pale fear in his face,
And counterfeits to die with her a space;
  Till manly shame bids him possess his breath,
  And live to be revengèd on her death.

The deep vexation of his inward soul
Hath served a dumb arrest upon his tongue;
Who, mad that sorrow should his use control,
Or keep him from heart-easing words so long,
Begins to talk; but through his lips do throng
  Weak words so thick, come in his poor heart's aid,
  That no man could distinguish what he said.

Yet sometime, "Tarquin," was pronouncèd plain,
But through his teeth, as if the name he tore.
This windy tempest, till it blow up rain,

Held back his sorrow's tide, to make it more;
At last it rains, and busy winds give o'er:
　Then son and father weep with equal strife
　Who should weep most, for daughter or for wife.

The one doth call her his, the other his,
Yet neither may possess the claim they lay.
The father says, "She's mine." "O, mine she is!"
Replies her husband: "do not take away
My sorrow's interest; let no mourner say
　He weeps for her, for she was only mine,
　And only must be wailed by Collatine."

"O," quoth Lucretius, "I did give that life
Which she too early and too late hath spilled!"
"Woe, woe," quoth Collatine, "she was my wife,
I owed her, and 'tis mine that she hath killed!"
"My daughter!" and "my wife!" with clamors filled
　The dispersed air, who, holding Lucrece' life,
　Answered their cries, "my daughter!" and "my wife!"

Brutus, who plucked the knife from Lucrece' side,
Seeing such emulation in their woe,
Began to clothe his wit in state and pride,
Burying in Lucrece' wound his folly's show.
He with the Romans was esteemèd so
　As silly-jeering idiots are with kings,
　For sportive words and uttering foolish things.

But now he throws that shallow habit by
Wherein deep policy did him disguise;
And armed his long-hid wits advisedly,
To check the tears in Collatinus' eyes.
"Thou wrongèd lord of Rome," quoth he, "arise;

Let my unsounded self, supposed a fool,
Now set thy long-experienced wit to school.

"Why, Collatine, is woe the cure for woe?
Do wounds help wounds, or grief help grievous deeds?
Is it revenge to give thyself a blow
For his foul act by whom thy fair wife bleeds?
Such childish humor from weak minds proceeds:
    Thy wretched wife mistook the matter so,
    To slay herself, that should have slain her foe.

"Courageous Roman, do not steep thy heart
In such relenting dew of lamentations,
But kneel with me, and help to bear thy part,
To rouse our Roman gods with invocations,
That they will suffer these abominations,
    Since Rome herself in them doth stand disgraced,
    By our strong arms from forth her fair streets chased.

"Now, by the Capitol that we adore,
And by this chaste blood so unjustly stained,
By heaven's fair sun that breeds the fat earth's store,
By all our country rights in Rome maintained,
And by chaste Lucrece' soul that late complained
    Her wrongs to us, and by this bloody knife,
    We will revenge the death of this true wife!"

This said, he struck his hand upon his breast,
And kissed the fatal knife to end his vow;
And to his protestation urged the rest,
Who, wond'ring at him, did his words allow:
Then jointly to the ground their knees they bow;
    And that deep vow, which Brutus made before,
    He doth again repeat, and that they swore.

When they had sworn to this advisèd doom,
They did conclude to bear dead Lucrece thence;
To show her bleeding body thorough Rome,
And so to publish Tarquin's foul offense:
Which being done with speedy diligence,
  The Romans plausibly did give consent
  To Tarquin's everlasting banishment.

Sonnets

TO THE ONLIE BEGETTER OF
THESE INSUING SONNETS
MR. W. H. ALL HAPPINESSE
AND THAT ETERNITIE
PROMISED BY
OUR EVER-LIVING POET
WISHETH
THE WELL-WISHING
ADVENTURER IN
SETTING
FORTH.
T. T.

1

From fairest creatures we desire increase,
That thereby beauty's rose might never die,
But as the riper should by time decease,
His tender heir might bear his memory:
But thou, contracted to thine own bright eyes,
Feed'st thy light's flame with self-substantial fuel,
Making a famine where abundance lies,
Thyself thy foe, to thy sweet self too cruel.
Thou that art now the world's fresh ornament,
And only herald to the gaudy spring,
Within thine own bud buriest thy content,
And, tender churl, mak'st waste in niggarding.
    Pity the world, or else this glutton be,
    To eat the world's due, by the grave and thee.

2

When forty winters shall besiege thy brow,
And dig deep trenches in thy beauty's field,
Thy youth's proud livery, so gazed on now,
Will be a tattered weed, of small worth held:
Then being asked where all thy beauty lies,
Where all the treasure of thy lusty days—
To say, within thine own deep-sunken eyes,
Were an all-eating shame and thriftless praise.
How much more praise deserved thy beauty's use,
If thou couldst answer—"This fair child of mine
Shall sum my count, and make my old excuse—"
Proving his beauty by succession thine!
    This were to be new-made when thou art old,
    And see thy blood warm when thou feel'st it cold.

3

Look in thy glass, and tell the face thou viewest,
Now is the time that face should form another;
Whose fresh repair if now thou not renewest,
Thou dost beguile the world, unbless some mother
For where is she so fair whose uneared womb
Disdains the tillage of thy husbandry?
Or who is he so fond will be the tomb
Of his self-love to stop posterity?
Thou art thy mother's glass, and she in thee
Calls back the lovely April of her prime:
So thou through windows of thine age shalt see,
Despite of wrinkles, this thy golden time.
    But if thou live, remembered not to be,
    Die single, and thine image dies with thee.

Unthrifty loveliness, why dost thou spend
Upon thyself thy beauty's legacy?
Nature's bequest gives nothing, but doth lend,
And, being frank, she lends to those are free.
Then, beauteous niggard, why dost thou abuse
The bounteous largess given thee to give?
Profitless usurer, why dost thou use
So great a sum of sums, yet canst not live?
For having traffic with thyself alone,
Thou of thyself thy sweet self dost deceive.
Then how, when nature calls thee to be gone,
What acceptable audit canst thou leave?
    Thy unused beauty must be tombed with thee,
    Which, usèd, lives th'executor to be.

Those hours, that with gentle work did frame
The lovely gaze where every eye doth dwell,
Will play the tyrants to the very same,
And that unfair which fairly doth excel;
For never-resting Time leads summer on
To hideous winter, and confounds him there;
Sap checked with frost, and lusty leaves quite gone,
Beauty o'ersnowed, and bareness everywhere:
Then, were not summer's distillation left,
A liquid prisoner pent in walls of glass,
Beauty's effect with beauty were bereft,
Nor it, nor no remembrance what it was:
 But flowers distilled, though they with winter meet,
 Leese but their show; their substance still lives sweet.

6

Then let not winter's ragged hand deface
In thee thy summer, ere thou be distilled:
Make sweet some vial; treasure thou some place
With beauty's treasure, ere it be self-killed.
That use is not forbidden usury,
Which happies those that pay the willing loan;
That's for thyself to breed another thee,
Or ten times happier, be it ten for one;
Ten times thyself were happier than thou art,
If ten of thine ten times refigured thee:
Then what could death do if thou shouldst depart,
Leaving thee living in posterity?
 Be not self-willed, for thou art much too fair
 To be Death's conquest, and make worms thine heir.

7

Lo, in the orient when the gracious light
Lifts up his burning head, each under eye
Doth homage to his new-appearing sight,
Serving with looks his sacred majesty;
And having climbed the steep-up heavenly hill,
Resembling strong youth in his middle age,
Yet mortal looks adore his beauty still,
Attending on his golden pilgrimage;
But when from highmost pitch, with weary car,
Like feeble age, he reeleth from the day,
The eyes, 'fore duteous, now converted are
From his low tract, and look another way:
    So thou, thyself outgoing in thy noon,
    Unlooked on diest, unless thou get a son.

8

Music to hear, why hear'st thou music sadly?
Sweets with sweets war not, joy delights in joy.
Why lov'st thou that which thou receiv'st not gladly,
Or else receiv'st with pleasure thine annoy?
If the true concord of well-tunèd sounds,
By unions married, do offend thine ear,
They do but sweetly chide thee, who confounds
In singleness the parts that thou shouldst bear.
Mark how one string, sweet husband to another,
Strikes each in each by mutual ordering;
Resembling sire and child and happy mother,
Who, all in one, one pleasing note do sing:
    Whose speechless song, being many, seeming one,
    Sings this to thee, "Thou single wilt prove none."

9

Is it for fear to wet a widow's eye
That thou consum'st thyself in single life?
Ah, if thou issueless shalt hap to die,
The world will wail thee, like a makeless wife;
The world will be thy widow, and still weep
That thou no form of thee hast left behind,
When every private widow well may keep,
By children's eyes, her husband's shape in mind.
Look, what an unthrift in the world doth spend
Shifts but his place, for still the world enjoys it;
But beauty's waste hath in the world an end,
And kept unused, the user so destroys it.
    No love toward others in that bosom sits
    That on himself such murd'rous shame commits.

10

For shame, deny that thou bear'st love to any,
Who for thyself art so unprovident.
Grant, if thou wilt, thou art beloved of many,
But that thou none lov'st is most evident;
For thou art so possessed with murd'rous hate,
That 'gainst thyself thou stick'st not to conspire,
Seeking that beauteous roof to ruinate,
Which to repair should be thy chief desire.
O, change thy thought, that I may change my mind!
Shall hate be fairer lodged than gentle love?
Be, as thy presence is, gracious and kind,
Or to thyself, at least, kindhearted prove:
    Make thee another self, for love of me,
    That beauty still may live in thine or thee.

11

As fast as thou shaft wane, so fast thou grow'st
In one of thine, from that which thou departest;
And that fresh blood which youngly thou bestow'st,
Thou mayst call thine, when thou from youth convertest.
Herein lives wisdom, beauty, and increase;
Without this, folly, age, and cold decay:
If all were minded so, the times should cease,
And threescore year would make the world away.
Let those whom Nature hath not made for store,
Harsh, featureless, and rude, barrenly perish:
Look, whom she best endowed, she gave thee more,
Which bounteous gift thou shouldst in bounty cherish;
    She carved thee for her seal, and meant thereby
    Thou shouldst print more, nor let that copy die.

12

When I do count the clock that tells the time,
And see the brave day sunk in hideous night;
When I behold the violet past prime,
And sable curls all silvered o'er with white;
When lofty trees I see barren of leaves,
Which erst from heat did canopy the herd,
And summer's green, all girded up in sheaves,
Borne on the bier with white and bristly beard;
Then of thy beauty do I question make,
That thou among the wastes of time must go,
Since sweets and beauties do themselves forsake,
And die as fast as they see others grow;
    And nothing 'gainst Time's scythe can make defense
    Save breed, to brave him when he takes thee hence.

13

O, that you were yourself! But, love, you are
No longer yours than you yourself here live:
Against this coming end you should prepare,
And your sweet semblance to some other give.
So should that beauty which you hold in lease
Find no determination; then you were
Yourself again, after yourself's decease,
When your sweet issue your sweet form should bear.
Who lets so fair a house fall to decay,
Which husbandry in honor might uphold
Against the stormy gusts of winter's day,
And barren rage of death's eternal cold?
  O, none but unthrifts! Dear my love, you know
  You had a father; let your son say so.

14

Not from the stars do I my judgment pluck;
And yet methinks I have astronomy,
But not to tell of good or evil luck,
Of plagues, of dearths, or seasons' quality:
Nor can I fortune to brief minutes tell,
Pointing to each his thunder, rain, and wind,
Or say with princes if it shall go well,
By oft predict that I in heaven find:
But from thine eyes my knowledge I derive,
And, constant stars, in them I read such art,
As truth and beauty shall together thrive.
If from thyself to store thou wouldst convert;
  Or else of thee this I prognosticate—
  Thy end is truth's and beauty's doom and date.

15

When I consider everything that grows
Holds in perfection but a little moment,
That this huge stage presenteth naught but shows
Whereon the stars in secret influence comment;
When I perceive that men as plants increase,
Cheerèd and checked even by the selfsame sky;
Vaunt in their youthful sap, at height decrease,
And wear their brave state out of memory;
Then the conceit of this inconstant stay
Sets you most rich in youth before my sight,
Where wasteful Time debateth with Decay,
To change your day of youth to sullied night;
    And, all in war with Time, for love of you,
    As he takes from you, I engraft you new.

16

But wherefore do not you a mightier way
Make war upon this bloody tyrant, Time?
And fortify yourself in your decay
With means more blessèd than my barren rhyme?
Now stand you on the top of happy hours;
And many maiden gardens, yet unset,
With virtuous wish would bear your living flowers,
Much liker than your painted counterfeit:
So should the lines of life that life repair,
Which this, Time's pencil, or my pupil pen,
Neither in inward worth nor outward fair,
Can make you live yourself in eyes of men.
    To give away yourself keeps yourself still;
    And you must live, drawn by your own sweet skill.

17

Who will believe my verse in time to come,
If it were filled with your most high deserts?
Though yet, heaven knows, it is but as a tomb
Which hides your life, and shows not half your parts.
If I could write the beauty of your eyes,
And in fresh numbers number all your graces,
The age to come would say, "This poet lies,
Such heavenly touches ne'er touched earthly faces."
So should my papers, yellowed with their age,
Be scorned, like old men of less truth than tongue;
And your true rights be termed a poet's rage,
And stretchèd meter of an antique song·
    But were some child of yours alive that time,
    You should live twice—in it, and in my rhyme.

18

Shall I compare thee to a summer's day?
Thou art more lovely and more temperate:
Rough winds do shake the darling buds of May,
And summer's lease hath all too short a date:
Sometime too hot the eye of heaven shines,
And often is his gold complexion dimmed;
And every fair from fair sometime declines,
By chance, or nature's changing course, untrimmed;
But thy eternal summer shall not fade,
Nor lose possession of that fair thou ow'st;
Nor shall Death brag thou wander'st in his shade,
When in eternal lines to time thou grow'st:
    So long as men can breathe, or eyes can see,
    So long lives this, and this gives life to thee.

19

Devouring Time, blunt thou the lion's paws,
And make the earth devour her own sweet brood;
Pluck the keen teeth from the fierce tiger's jaws,
And burn the long-lived phoenix in her blood;
Make glad and sorry seasons as thou fleets,
And do whate'er thou wilt, swift-footed Time,
To the wide world and all her fading sweets;
But I forbid thee one most heinous crime:
O, carve not with thy hours my love's fair brow,
Nor draw no lines there with thine antique pen;
Him in thy course untainted do allow,
For beauty's pattern to succeeding men.
    Yet, do thy worst, old Time: despite thy wrong,
    My love shall in my verse ever live young.

20

A woman's face, with Nature's own hand painted,
Hast thou, the master-mistress of my passion;
A woman's gentle heart, but not acquainted
With shifting change, as is false women's fashion;
An eye more bright than theirs, less false in rolling,
Gilding the object whereupon it gazeth;
A man in hue, all hues in his controlling,
Which steals men's eyes, and women's souls amazeth.
And for a woman wert thou first created;
Till Nature, as she wrought thee, fell a-doting,
And, by addition, me of thee defeated,
By adding one thing to my purpose nothing.
    But since she pricked thee out for women's pleasure,
    Mine be thy love, and thy love's use their treasure.

21

So is it not with me as with that Muse,
Stirred by a painted beauty to his verse;
Who heaven itself for ornament doth use,
And every fair with his fair doth rehearse;
Making a couplement of proud compare,
With sun and moon, with earth and sea's rich gems,
With April's firstborn flowers, and all things rare
That heaven's air in this huge rondure hems.
O, let me, true in love, but truly write,
And then believe me, my love is as fair
As any mother's child, though not so bright
As those gold candles fixed in heaven's air.
　　Let them say more that like of hearsay well;
　　I will not praise that purpose not to sell.

22

My glass shall not persuade me I am old,
So long as youth and thou are of one date;
But when in thee Time's furrows I behold,
Then look I death my days should expiate.
For all that beauty that doth cover thee
Is but the seemly raiment of my heart,
Which in thy breast doth live, as thine in me:
How can I, then, be elder than thou art?
O, therefore, love, be of thyself so wary,
As I, not for myself, but for thee will;
Bearing thy heart, which I will keep so chary
As tender nurse her babe from faring ill.
　　Presume not on thy heart when mine is slain;
　　Thou gav'st me thine, not to give back again.

23

As an unperfect actor on the stage,
Who with his fear is put besides his part,
Or some fierce thing replete with too much rage,
Whose strength's abundance weakens his own heart;
So I, for fear of trust, forget to say
The perfect ceremony of love's rite,
And in mine own love's strength seem to decay,
O'ercharged with burden of mine own love's might.
O, let my books be, then, the eloquence
And dumb presagers of my speaking breast;
Who plead for love, and look for recompense,
More than that tongue that more hath more expressed.
    O, learn to read what silent love hath writ:
    To hear with eyes belongs to love's fine wit.

24

Mine eye hath played the painter, and hath stelled
Thy beauty's form in table of my heart;
My body is the frame wherein 'tis held,
And perspective it is best painter's art.
For through the painter must you see his skill,
To find where your true image pictured lies,
Which in my bosom's shop is hanging still,
That hath his windows glazèd with thine eyes.
Now see what good turns eyes for eyes have done;
Mine eyes have drawn thy shape, and thine for me
Are windows to my breast, wherethrough the sun
Delights to peep, to gaze therein on thee;
        Yet eyes this cunning want to grace their art,
        They draw but what they see, know not the heart.

25

Let those who are in favor with their stars,
Of public honor and proud titles boast,
Whilst I, whom fortune of such triumph bars,
Unlooked for joy in that I honor most.
Great princes' favorites their fair leaves spread
But as the marigold at the sun's eye;
And in themselves their pride lies buried,
For at a frown they in their glory die.
The painful warrior famousèd for fight,
After a thousand victories once foil'd,
Is from the book of honor razèd quite,
And all the rest forgot for which he toiled:
    Then happy I, that love and am beloved
    Where I may not remove nor be removed.

26

Lord of my love, to whom in vassalage
Thy merit hath my duty strongly knit,
To thee I send this written embassage,
To witness duty, not to show my wit;
Duty so great, which wit so poor as mine
May make seem bare, in wanting words to show it;
But that I hope some good conceit of thine
In thy soul's thought, all naked, will bestow it;
Till whatsoever star that guides by moving,
Points on me graciously with fair aspect,
And puts apparel on my tatter'd loving,
To show me worthy of thy sweet respect:
    Then may I dare to boast how I do love thee;
    Till then not show my head where thou mayst prove me.

27

Weary with toil, I haste me to my bed,
The dear repose for limbs with travel tired;
But then begins a journey in my head,
To work my mind, when body's work's expired:
For then my thoughts (from far where I abide)
Intend a zealous pilgrimage to thee,
And keep my drooping eyelids open wide,
Looking on darkness which the blind do see:
Save that my soul's imaginary sight
Presents thy shadow to my sightless view,
Which, like a jewel hung in ghastly night,
Makes black night beauteous, and her old face new.
    Lo, thus, by day my limbs, by night my mind,
    For thee and for myself no quiet find.

28

How can I, then, return in happy plight,
That am debarred the benefit of rest?
When day's oppression is not eased by night,
But day by night, and night by day, oppressed?
And each, though enemies to either's reign,
Do in consent shake hands to torture me;
The one by toil, the other to complain
How far I toil, still farther off from thee.
I tell the day, to please him, thou art bright,
And dost him grace when clouds do blot the heaven:
So flatter I the swart-complexioned night,
When sparkling stars twire not, thou gild'st the even.
    But day doth daily draw my sorrows longer,
    And night doth nightly make grief's strength seem
        stronger.

29

When in disgrace with Fortune and men's eyes,
I all alone beweep my outcast state,
And trouble deaf heaven with my bootless cries,
And look upon myself, and curse my fate,
Wishing me like to one more rich in hope,
Featured like him, like him with friends possessed,
Desiring this man's art, and that man's scope,
With what I most enjoy contented least;
Yet in these thoughts myself almost despising,
Haply I think on thee—and then my state
(Like to the lark at break of day arising
From sullen earth) sings hymns at heaven's gate;
    For thy sweet love remembered such wealth brings,
    That then I scorn to change my state with kings.

30

When to the sessions of sweet silent thought
I summon up remembrance of things past,
I sigh the lack of many a thing I sought,
And with old woes new wail my dear time's waste:
Then can I drown an eye, unused to flow,
For precious friends hid in death's dateless night,
And weep afresh Love's long-since-canceled woe,
And moan th'expense of many a vanished sight:
Then can I grieve at grievances foregone,
And heavily from woe to woe tell o'er
The sad account of fore-bemoanèd moan,
Which I new pay as if not paid before.
    But if the while I think on thee, dear friend,
    All losses are restored, and sorrows end.

31

Thy bosom is endearèd with all hearts,
Which I by lacking have supposèd dead;
And there reigns love, and all love's loving parts,
And all those friends which I thought burièd.
How many a holy and obsequious tear
Hath dear-religious love stolen from mine eye,
As interest of the dead, which now appear
But things removed, that hidden in thee lie!
Thou art the grave where buried love doth live,
Hung with the trophies of my lovers gone,
Who all their parts of me to thee did give;
That due of many now is thine alone:
    Their images I loved I view in thee,
    And thou, all they, hast all-the-all of me.

32

If thou survive my well-contented day,
When that churl Death my bones with dust shall cover,
And shalt by fortune once more resurvey
These poor rude lines of thy deceasèd lover,
Compare them with the bettering of the time;
And though they be outstripped by every pen,
Reserve them for my love, not for their rhyme,
Exceeded by the height of happier men.
O, then vouchsafe me but this loving thought—
"Had my friend's Muse grown with this growing age,
A dearer birth than this his love had brought,
To march in ranks of better equipage:
    But since he died, and poets better prove,
    Theirs for their style I'll read, his for his love."

33

Full many a glorious morning have I seen
Flatter the mountaintops with sovereign eye,
Kissing with golden face the meadows green,
Gilding pale streams with heavenly alchemy;
Anon permit the basest clouds to ride
With ugly rack on his celestial face,
And from the forlorn world his visage hide,
Stealing unseen to west with this disgrace:
Even so my sun one early morn did shine
With all triumphant splendor on my brow,
But, out, alack, he was but one hour mine,
The region cloud hath masked him from me now.
    Yet him for this my love no whit disdaineth;
    Suns of the world may stain when heaven's sun staineth.

34

Why didst thou promise such a beauteous day,
And make me travel forth without my cloak,
To let base clouds o'ertake me in my way,
Hiding thy brav'ry in their rotten smoke?
'Tis not enough that through the cloud thou break,
To dry the rain on my storm-beaten face,
For no man well of such a salve can speak,
That heals the wound, and cures not the disgrace:
Nor can thy shame give physic to my grief;
Though thou repent, yet I have still the loss:
Th'offender's sorrow lends but weak relief
To him that bears the strong offense's cross.
    Ah, but those tears are pearl which thy love sheds,
    And they are rich, and ransom all ill deeds.

35

No more be grieved at that which thou hast done:
Roses have thorns, and silver fountains mud;
Clouds and eclipses stain both moon and sun,
And loathsome canker lives in sweetest bud.
All men make faults, and even I in this,
Authorizing thy trespass with compare,
Myself corrupting, salving thy amiss,
Excusing thy sins more than thy sins are:
For to thy sensual fault I bring in sense—
Thy adverse party is thy advocate—
And 'gainst myself a lawful plea commence:
Such civil war is in my love and hate,
    That I an accessory needs must be
    To that sweet thief which sourly robs from me.

36

Let me confess that we two must be twain,
Although our undivided loves are one;
So shall those blots that do with me remain,
Without thy help, by me be borne alone.
In our two loves there is but one respect,
Though in our lives a separable spite,
Which though it alter not love's sole effect,
Yet doth it steal sweet hours from love's delight.
I may not evermore acknowledge thee,
Lest my bewailèd guilt should do thee shame;
Nor thou with public kindness honor me,
Unless thou take that honor from thy name:
    But do not so; I love thee in such sort,
    As, thou being mine, mine is thy good report.

37

As a decrepit father takes delight
To see his active child do deeds of youth,
So I, made lame by Fortune's dearest spite,
Take all my comfort of thy worth and truth;
For whether beauty, birth, or wealth, or wit,
Or any of these all, or all, or more,
Entitled in thy parts do crownèd sit,
I make my love engrafted to this store:
So then I am not lame, poor, nor despised,
Whilst that this shadow doth such substance give,
That I in thy abundance am sufficed,
And by a part of all thy glory live.
    Look what is best, that best I wish in thee;
    This wish I have; then ten times happy me!

How can my Muse want subject to invent,
While thou dost breathe, that pour'st into my verse
Thine own sweet argument, too excellent
For every vulgar paper to rehearse?
O, give thyself the thanks, if aught in me
Worthy perusal stand against thy sight;
For who's so dumb that cannot write to thee,
When thou thyself dost give invention light?
Be thou the tenth Muse, ten times more in worth
Than those old nine which rhymers invocate;
And he that calls on thee, let him bring forth
Eternal numbers to outlive long date.
    If my slight Muse do please these curious days,
    The pain be mine, but thine shall be the praise.

O, how thy worth with manners may I sing,
When thou art all the better part of me?
What can mine own praise to mine own self bring?
And what is't but mine own, when I praise thee?
Even for this let us divided live,
And our dear love lose name of single one,
That by this separation I may give
That due to thee, which thou deserv'st alone.
O absence, what a torment wouldst thou prove,
Were it not thy sour leisure gave sweet leave
To entertain the time with thoughts of love—
Which time and thoughts so sweetly doth deceive—
    And that thou teachest how to make one twain,
    By praising him here who doth hence remain!

40

Take all my loves, my love, yea, take them all;
What hast thou then more than thou hadst before?
No love, my love, that thou mayst true love call;
All mine was thine before thou hadst this more.
Then, if for my love thou my love receivest,
I cannot blame thee for my love thou usest;
But yet be blamed, if thou thyself deceivest
By willful taste of what thyself refusest.
I do forgive thy robb'ry, gentle thief,
Although thou steal thee all my poverty;
And yet, love knows, it is a greater grief
To bear love's wrong, than hate's known injury.
    Lascivious grace, in whom all ill well shows,
    Kill me with spites; yet we must not be foes.

41

Those pretty wrongs that liberty commits
When I am sometime absent from thy heart,
Thy beauty and thy years full well befits,
For still temptation follows where thou art.
Gentle thou art, and therefore to be won,
Beauteous thou art, therefore to be assailed;
And when a woman woos, what woman's son
Will sourly leave her till she have prevailed?
Ah me, but yet thou mightst my seat forbear,
And chide thy beauty and thy straying youth,
Who lead thee in their riot even there
Where thou art forced to break a twofold truth—
    Hers, by thy beauty tempting her to thee,
    Thine, by thy beauty being false to me.

42

That thou hast her, it is not all my grief,
And yet it may be said I loved her dearly;
That she hath thee, is of my wailing chief,
A loss in love that touches me more nearly.
Loving offenders, thus I will excuse ye—
Thou dost love her, because thou know'st I love her;
And for my sake even so doth she abuse me,
Suff'ring my friend for my sake to approve her.
If I lose thee, my loss is my love's gain,
And losing her, my friend hath found that loss;
Both find each other, and I lose both twain,
And both for my sake lay on me this cross:
    But here's the joy—my friend and I are one;
    Sweet flatt'ry! Then she loves but me alone.

43

When most I wink, then do mine eyes best see,
For all the day they view things unrespected;
But when I sleep, in dreams they look on thee,
And, darkly bright, are bright in dark directed.
Then thou, whose shadow shadows doth make bright,
How would thy shadow's form form happy show,
To the clear day with thy much clearer light,
When to unseeing eyes thy shade shines so!
How would, I say, mine eyes be blessèd made
By looking on thee in the living day,
When in dead night thy fair imperfect shade
Through heavy sleep on sightless eyes doth stay!
    All days are nights to see till I see thee,
    And nights, bright days when dreams do show thee me.

44

If the dull substance of my flesh were thought,
Injurious distance should not stop my way;
For then, despite of space, I would be brought
From limits far remote, where thou dost stay.
No matter then although my foot did stand
Upon the farthest earth removed from thee;
For nimble thought can jump both sea and land,
As soon as think the place where he would be.
But, ah, thought kills me, that I am not thought,
To leap large lengths of miles when thou art gone,
But that, so much of earth and water wrought,
I must attend time's leisure with my moan;
    Receiving naught by elements so slow
    But heavy tears, badges of either's woe.

45

The other two, slight air and purging fire,
Are both with thee, wherever I abide;
The first my thought, the other my desire,
These present-absent with swift motion slide.
For when these quicker elements are gone
In tender embassy of love to thee,
My life, being made of four, with two alone
Sinks down to death, oppressed with melancholy;
Until life's composition be recurred
By those swift messengers returned from thee,
Who even but now come back again, assured
Of thy fair health, recounting it to me:
    This told, I joy; but then no longer glad,
    I send them back again, and straight grow sad.

46

Mine eye and heart are at a mortal war,
How to divide the conquest of thy sight;
Mine eye my heart thy picture's sight would bar,
My heart mine eye the freedom of that right.
My heart doth plead that thou in him dost lie——
A closet never pierced with crystal eyes——
But the defendant doth that plea deny,
And says in him thy fair appearance lies.
To 'cide this title is impannellèd
A quest of thoughts, all tenants to the heart;
And by their verdict is determinèd
The clear eye's moiety and the dear heart's part:
    As thus—mine eye's due is thine outward part,
    And my heart's right thine inward love of heart.

47

Betwixt mine eye and heart a league is took,
And each doth good turns now unto the other:
When that mine eye is famished for a look,
Or heart in love with sighs himself doth smother,
With my love's picture then my eye doth feast,
And to the painted banquet bids my heart;
Another time mine eye is my heart's guest,
And in his thoughts of love doth share a part:
So, either by thy picture or my love,
Thyself away art present still with me;
For thou not farther than my thoughts canst move,
And I am still with them, and they with thee;
 Or, if they sleep, thy picture in my sight
 Awakes my heart to heart's and eye's delight.

48

How careful was I, when I took my way,
Each trifle under truest bars to thrust,
That to my use it might unusèd stay
From hands of falsehood, in sure wards of trust
But thou, to whom my jewels trifles are,
Most worthy comfort, now my greatest grief,
Thou, best of dearest, and mine only care,
Art left the prey of every vulgar thief.
Thee have I not locked up in any chest,
Save where thou art not, though I feel thou art,
Within the gentle closure of my breast,
From whence at pleasure thou mayst come and part;
 And even thence thou wilt be stolen I fear,
 For truth proves thievish for a prize so dear.

49

Against that time, if ever that time come,
When I shall see thee frown on my defects,
Whenas thy love hath cast his utmost sum,
Called to that audit by advised respects;
Against that time, when thou shalt strangely pass,
And scarcely greet me with that sun, thine eye,
When love, converted from the thing it was,
Shall reasons find of settled gravity—
Against that time do I ensconce me here
Within the knowledge of mine own desert,
And this my hand against myself uprear,
To guard the lawful reasons on thy part:
    To leave poor me thou hast the strength of laws,
    Since why to love I can allege no cause.

50

How heavy do I journey on the way,
When what I seek—my weary travel's end—
Doth teach that ease and that repose to say,
"Thus far the miles are measured from thy friend!"
The beast that bears me, tired with my woe,
Plods dully on, to bear that weight in me,
As if by some instinct the wretch did know
His rider loved not speed, being made from thee:
The bloody spur cannot provoke him on
That sometimes anger thrusts into his hide,
Which heavily he answers with a groan,
More sharp to me than spurring to his side;
    For that same groan doth put this in my mind—
    My grief lies onward, and my joy behind.

51

Thus can my love excuse the slow offense
Of my dull bearer when from thee I speed:
From where thou art why should I haste me thence?
Till I return, of posting is no need.
O, what excuse will my poor beast then find,
When swift extremity can seem but slow?
Then should I spur, though mounted on the wind,
In wingèd speed no motion shall I know:
Then can no horse with my desire keep pace;
Therefore desire, of perfect'st love being made,
Shall neigh—no dull flesh—in his fiery race;
But love, for love, thus shall excuse my jade—
    Since from thee going he went willful slow,
    Towards thee I'll run, and give him leave to go.

52

So am I as the rich, whose blessèd key
Can bring him to his sweet up-lockèd treasure,
The which he will not every hour survey,
For blunting the fine point of seldom pleasure.
Therefore are feasts so solemn and so rare,
Since, seldom coming, in the long year set,
Like stones of worth they thinly placèd are,
Or captain jewels in the carcanet.
So is the time that keeps you, as my chest,
Or as the wardrobe which the robe doth hide,
To make some special instant special blest,
By new unfolding his imprisoned pride.
    Blessèd are you, whose worthiness gives scope,
    Being had, to triumph, being lacked, to hope.

53

What is your substance, whereof are you made,
That millions of strange shadows on you tend?
Since everyone hath, every one, one shade,
And you, but one, can every shadow lend.
Describe Adonis, and the counterfeit
Is poorly imitated after you;
On Helen's cheek all art of beauty set,
And you in Grecian tires are painted new:
Speak of the spring, and foison of the year;
The one doth shadow of your beauty show,
The other as your bounty doth appear;
And you in every blessèd shape we know.
    In all external grace you have some part,
    But you like none, none you, for constant heart.

54

O, how much more doth beauty beauteous seem
By that sweet ornament which truth doth give!
The rose looks fair, but fairer we it deem
For that sweet odor which doth in it live.
The canker blooms have full as deep a dye
As the perfumèd tincture of the roses,
Hang on such thorns, and play as wantonly
When summer's breath their maskèd buds discloses:
But, for their virtue only is their show,
They live unwooed, and unrespected fade;
Die to themselves. Sweet roses do not so;
Of their sweet deaths are sweetest odors made:
    And so of you, beauteous and lovely youth,
    When that shall fade, by verse distills your truth.

55

Not marble nor the gilded monuments
Of princes, shall outlive this powerful rhyme;
But you shall shine more bright in these contents
Than unswept stone, besmeared with sluttish time.
When wasteful war shall statues overturn,
And broils root out the work of masonry,
Nor Mars his sword nor war's quick fire shall burn
The living record of your memory.
'Gainst death and all oblivious enmity
Shall you pace forth; your praise shall still find room,
Even in the eyes of all posterity
That wear this world out to the ending doom.
    So, till the judgment that yourself arise,
    You live in this, and dwell in lovers' eyes.

56

Sweet love, renew thy force; be it not said
Thy edge should blunter be than appetite,
Which but today by feeding is allayed,
Tomorrow sharpened in his former might:
So, love, be thou: although today thou fill
Thy hungry eyes, even till they wink with fullness,
Tomorrow see again, and do not kill
The spirit of love with a perpetual dullness.
Let this sad interim like the ocean be
Which parts the shore, where two contracted new
Come daily to the banks, that, when they see
Return of love, more blest may be the view;
    Or call it winter, which, being full of care,
    Makes summer's welcome thrice more wished,
        more rare.

57

Being your slave, what should I do but tend
Upon the hours and times of your desire?
I have no precious time at all to spend,
Nor services to do, till you require.
Nor dare I chide the world-without-end hour,
Whilst I, my sovereign, watch the clock for you,
Nor think the bitterness of absence sour,
When you have bid your servant once adieu,
Nor dare I question with my jealous thought
Where you may be, or your affairs suppose,
But, like a sad slave, stay and think of naught
Save, where you are how happy you make those.
    So true a fool is love, that in your will,
    Though you do anything, he thinks no ill.

58

That god forbid that made me first your slave,
I should in thought control your times of pleasure,
Or at your hand th'account of hours to crave,
Being your vassal, bound to stay your leisure!
O, let me suffer, being at your beck,
Th'imprison'd absence of your liberty;
And patience, tame to sufferance, bide each cheek,
Without accusing you of injury.
Be where you list, your charter is so strong,
That you yourself may privilege your time:
Do what you will, to you it doth belong
Yourself to pardon of self-doing crime.
    I am to wait, though waiting so be hell;
    Not blame your pleasure, be it ill or well.

59

If there be nothing new, but that which is
Hath been before, how are our brains beguiled,
Which, laboring for invention, bear amiss
The second burden of a former child!
O, that record could with a backward look,
Even of five hundred courses of the sun,
Show me your image in some antique book,
Since mind at first in character was done!
That I might see what the old world could say
To this composèd wonder of your frame;
Whether we are mended, or whe'er better they,
Or whether revolution be the same.
    O, sure I am, the wits of former days
    To subjects worse have given admiring praise!

60

Like as the waves make towards the pebbled shore,
So do our minutes hasten to their end;
Each changing place with that which goes before,
In sequent toil all forwards do contend.
Nativity, once in the main of light,
Crawls to maturity, wherewith being crowned,
Crookèd eclipses 'gainst his glory fight,
And Time, that gave, doth now his gift confound.
Time doth transfix the flourish set on youth,
And delves the parallels in beauty's brow;
Feeds on the rarities of nature's truth,
And nothing stands but for his scythe to mow:
    And yet, to times in hope my verse shall stand,
    Praising thy worth, despite his cruel hand.

61

Is it thy will thy image should keep open
My heavy eyelids to the weary night?
Dost thou desire my slumbers should be broken
While shadows like to thee do mock my sight?
Is it thy spirit that thou send'st from thee
So far from home into my deeds to pry,
To find out shames and idle hours in me,
The scope and tenor of thy jealousy?
O, no! thy love, though much, is not so great;
It is my love that keeps mine eye awake;
Mine own true love that doth my rest defeat,
To play the watchman ever for thy sake:
    For thee watch I whilst thou dost wake elsewhere,
    From me far off, with others all too near.

62

Sin of self-love possesseth all mine eye,
And all my soul, and all my every part;
And for this sin there is no remedy,
It is so grounded inward in my heart.
Methinks no face so gracious is as mine,
No shape so true, no truth of such account;
And for myself mine own worth do define,
As I all other in all worths surmount.
But when my glass shows me myself indeed,
Beated and chopped with tanned antiquity,
Mine own self-love quite contrary I read;
Self so self-loving were iniquity.
    'Tis thee (myself) that for myself I praise,
    Painting my age with beauty of thy days.

63

Against my love shall be, as I am now,
With Time's injurious hand crushed and o'erworn;
When hours have drained his blood, and filled his brow
With lines and wrinkles; when his youthful morn
Hath traveled on to Age's steepy night;
And all those beauties whereof now he's king
Are vanishing or vanished out of sight,
Stealing away the treasure of his spring;
For such a time do I now fortify
Against confounding age's cruel knife,
That he shall never cut from memory
My sweet love's beauty, though my lover's life:
    His beauty shall in these black lines be seen,
    And they shall live, and he in them, still green.

64

When I have seen by Time's fell hand defaced
The rich-proud cost of outworn buried age;
When sometime lofty towers I see down-razed,
And brass eternal slave to mortal rage;
When I have seen the hungry ocean gain
Advantage on the kingdom of the shore,
And the firm soil win of the wat'ry main,
Increasing store with loss, and loss with store;
When I have seen such interchange of state,
Or state itself confounded to decay;
Ruin hath taught me thus to ruminate—
That Time will come and take my love away.
    This thought is as a death, which cannot choose
    But weep to have that which it fears to lose.

65

Since brass, nor stone, nor earth, nor boundless sea,
But sad mortality o'ersways their power,
How with this rage shall beauty hold a plea,
Whose action is no stronger than a flower?
O, how shall summer's honey breath hold out
Against the wreckful siege of battering days,
When rocks impregnable are not so stout,
Nor gates of steel so strong, but Time decays?
O fearful meditation! Where, alack!
Shall Time's best jewel from Time's chest lie hid?
Or what strong hand can hold his swift foot back?
Or who his spoil of beauty can forbid?
    O, none, unless this miracle have might,
    That in black ink my love may still shine bright.

66

Tired with all these, for restful death I cry—
As, to behold desert a beggar born,
And needy nothing trimmed in jollity,
And purest faith unhappily forsworn,
And gilded honor shamefully misplaced,
And maiden virtue rudely strumpeted,
And right perfection wrongfully disgraced,
And strength by limping sway disablèd,
And art made tongue-tied by authority,
And folly, doctor-like, controlling skill,
And simple truth miscalled simplicity,
And captive good attending captain ill—
    Tired with all these, from these would I be gone,
    Save that, to die, I leave my love alone.

67

Ah, wherefore with infection should he live,
And with his presence grace impiety,
That sin by him advantage should achieve,
And lace itself with his society?
Why should false painting imitate his cheek,
And steal dead seeming of his living hue?
Why should poor beauty indirectly seek
Roses of shadow, since his rose is true?
Why should he live, now Nature bankrupt is,
Beggared of blood to blush through lively veins?
For she hath no exchequer now but his,
And, proud of many, lives upon his gains.
    O, him she stores, to show what wealth she had
    In days long since, before these last so bad.

68

Thus is his cheek the map of days outworn,
When beauty lived and died as flowers do now,
Before these bastard signs of fair were born,
Or durst inhabit on a living brow;
Before the golden tresses of the dead,
The right of sepulchers, were shorn away,
To live a second life on second head;
Ere beauty's dead fleece made another gay:
In him those holy antique hours are seen,
Without all ornament, itself, and true,
Making no summer of another's green,
Robbing no old to dress his beauty new;
    And him as for a map doth Nature store,
    To show false Art what beauty was of yore.

69

Those parts of thee that the world's eye doth view
Want nothing that the thought of hearts can mend;
All tongues, the voice of souls, give thee that due,
Uttering bare truth, even so as foes commend.
Thy outward thus with outward praise is crowned;
But those same tongues that give thee so thine own,
In other accents do this praise confound,
By seeing farther than the eye hath shown.
They look into the beauty of thy mind,
And that, in guess, they measure by thy deeds;
Then, churls, their thoughts, although their eyes were kind,
To thy fair flower add the rank smell of weeds:
But why thy odor matcheth not thy show,
The soil is this—that thou dost common grow.

70

That thou art blamed shall not be thy defect,
For slander's mark was ever yet the fair;
The ornament of beauty is suspect,
A crow that flies in heaven's sweetest air.
So thou be good, slander doth but approve
Thy worth the greater, being wooed of time;
For canker vice the sweetest buds doth love,
And thou present'st a pure unstainèd prime.
Thou hast passed by the ambush of young days,
Either not assailed, or victor being charged;
Yet this thy praise cannot be so thy praise,
To tie up envy evermore enlarged:
If some suspect of ill masked not thy show,
Then thou alone kingdoms of hearts shouldst owe.

71

No longer mourn for me when I am dead
Than you shall hear the surly sullen bell
Give warning to the world that I am fled
From this vile world, with vilest worms to dwell:
Nay, if you read this line, remember not
The hand that writ it; for I love you so,
That I in your sweet thoughts would be forgot,
If thinking on me then should make you woe.
Oh, if, I say, you look upon this verse
When I perhaps compounded am with clay,
Do not so much as my poor name rehearse;
But let your love even with my life decay;
    Lest the wise world should look into your moan,
    And mock you with me after I am gone.

72

O, lest the world should task you to recite
What merit lived in me that you should love,
After my death, dear love, forget me quite;
For you in me can nothing worthy prove
Unless you would devise some virtuous lie,
To do more for me than mine own desert,
And hang more praise upon deceasèd I
Than niggard truth would willingly impart:
O, lest your true love may seem false in this,
That you for love speak well of me untrue,
My name be buried where my body is,
And live no more to shame nor me nor you.
    For I am shamed by that which I bring forth,
    And so should you, to love things nothing worth.

73

That time of year thou mayst in me behold
When yellow leaves, or none, or few, do hang
Upon those boughs which shake against the cold,
Bare ruined choirs, where late the sweet birds sang.
In me thou see'st the twilight of such day
As after sunset fadeth in the west;
Which by and by black night doth take away,
Death's second self, that seals up all in rest.
In me thou see'st the glowing of such fire,
That on the ashes of his youth doth lie,
As the deathbed whereon it must expire,
Consumed with that which it was nourished by.
　　This thou perceiv'st, which makes thy love more strong,
　　To love that well which thou must leave ere long.

74

But be contented: when that fell arrest
Without all bail shall carry me away,
My life hath in this line some interest,
Which for memorial still with thee shall stay.
When thou reviewest this, thou dost review
The very part was consecrate to thee:
The earth can have but earth, which is his due;
My spirit is thine, the better part of me:
So, then, thou hast but lost the dregs of life,
The prey of worms, my body being dead;
The coward conquest of a wretch's knife,
Too base of thee to be rememberèd.
　　The worth of that, is that which it contains,
　　And that is this, and this with thee remains.

75

So are you to my thoughts as food to life,
Or as sweet-seasoned showers are to the ground;
And for the peace of you I hold such strife
As 'twixt a miser and his wealth is found;
Now proud as an enjoyer, and anon
Doubting the filching age will steal his treasure;
Now counting best to be with you alone,
Then bettered that the world may see my pleasure:
Sometime all full with feasting on your sight,
And by and by clean starvèd for a look;
Possessing or pursuing no delight,
Save what is had or must from you be took.
    Thus do I pine and surfeit day by day,
    Or gluttoning on all, or all away.

76

Why is my verse so barren of new pride,
So far from variation or quick change?
Why, with the time, do I not glance aside
To newfound methods and to compounds strange?
Why write I still all one, ever the same,
And keep invention in a noted weed,
That every word doth almost tell my name,
Showing their birth, and where they did proceed?
O, know, sweet love, I always write of you,
And you and love are still my argument;
So all my best is dressing old words new,
Spending again what is already spent:
    For as the sun is daily new and old,
    So is my love still telling what is told.

77

Thy glass will show thee how thy beauties wear,
Thy dial how thy precious minutes waste;
The vacant leaves thy mind's imprint will bear,
And of this book this learning mayst thou taste.
The wrinkles which thy glass will truly show,
Of mouthèd graves will give thee memory;
Thou by thy dial's shady stealth mayst know
Time's thievish progress to eternity
Look, what thy memory cannot contain,
Commit to these waste blanks, and thou shalt find
Those children nursed, delivered from thy brain,
To take a new acquaintance of thy mind.
    These offices, so oft as thou wilt look,
    Shall profit thee, and much enrich thy book.

78

So oft have I invoked thee for my Muse,
And found such fair assistance in my verse,
As every alien pen hath got my use,
And under thee their poesy disperse.
Thine eyes, that taught the dumb on high to sing,
And heavy ignorance aloft to fly,
Have added feathers to the learnèd's wing,
And given grace a double majesty.
Yet be most proud of that which I compile,
Whose influence is thine, and born of thee:
In others' works thou dost but mend the style,
And arts with thy sweet graces gracèd be;
    But thou art all my art, and dost advance
    As high as learning my rude ignorance.

79

Whilst I alone did call upon thy aid,
My verse alone had all thy gentle grace;
But now my gracious numbers are decayed,
And my sick Muse doth give another place.
I grant, sweet love, thy lovely argument
Deserves the travail of a worthier pen;
Yet what of thee thy poet doth invent,
He robs thee of, and pays it thee again.
He lends thee virtue, and he stole that word
From thy behavior; beauty doth he give,
And found it in thy cheek; he can afford
No praise to thee but what in thee doth live.
    Then thank him not for that which he doth say,
    Since what he owes thee thou thyself dost pay.

80

O, how I faint when I of you do write,
Knowing a better spirit doth use your name,
And in the praise thereof spends all his might,
To make me tongue-tied, speaking of your fame!
But since your worth, wide as the ocean is,
The humble as the proudest sail doth bear,
My saucy bark, inferior far to his,
On your broad main doth willfully appear.
Your shallowest help will hold me up afloat,
Whilst he upon your soundless deep doth ride;
Or, being wrecked, I am a worthless boat,
He of tall building and of goodly pride:
    Then if he thrive, and I be cast away,
    The worst was this—my love was my decay.

81

Or I shall live your epitaph to make,
Or you survive when I in earth am rotten;
From hence your memory death cannot take,
Although in me each part will be forgotten.
Your name from hence immortal life shall have,
Though I, once gone, to all the world must die:
The earth can yield me but a common grave,
When you entombèd in men's eyes shall lie.
Your monument shall be my gentle verse,
Which eyes not yet created shall o'er-read;
And tongues to be your being shall rehearse,
When all the breathers of this world are dead;
      You still shall live—such virtue hath my pen—
      Where breath most breathes—even in the mouths
         of men.

82

I grant thou wert not married to my Muse,
And therefore mayst without attaint o'erlook
The dedicated words which writers use
Of their fair subject, blessing every book.
Thou art as fair in knowledge as in hue,
Finding thy worth a limit past my praise;
And therefore art enforced to seek anew
Some fresher stamp of the time-bettering days.
And do so, love; yet when they have devised
What strainèd touches rhetoric can lend,
Thou truly fair wert truly sympathized
In true-plain words, by thy true-telling friend;
      And their gross painting might be better used
      Where cheeks need blood—in thee it is abused.

83

I never saw that you did painting need,
And therefore to your fair no painting set;
I found, or thought I found, you did exceed
The barren tender of a poet's debt:
And therefore have I slept in your report,
That you yourself, being extant, well might show
How far a modern quill doth come too short,
Speaking of worth, what worth in you doth grow.
This silence for my sin you did impute,
Which shall be most my glory, being dumb;
For I impair not beauty, being mute,
When others would give life, and bring a tomb.
    There lives more life in one of your fair eyes
    Than both your poets can in praise devise.

84

Who is it that says most which can say more
Than this rich praise—that you alone are you?
In whose confine immurèd is the store
Which should example where your equal grew?
Lean penury within that pen doth dwell,
That to his subject lends not some small glory;
But he that writes of you, if he can tell
That you arc you, so dignifies his story.
Let him but copy what in you is writ,
Not making worse what nature made so clear,
And such a counterpart shall fame his wit,
Making his style admirèd everywhere.
    You to your beauteous blessings add a curse,
    Being fond on praise, which makes your praises worse.

85

My tongue-tied Muse in manners holds her still,
While comments of your praise, richly compiled,
Reserve their character with golden quill,
And precious phrase by all the Muses filed.
I think good thoughts, whilst others write good words,
And, like unlettered clerk, still cry "Amen"
To every hymn that able spirit affords,
In polished form of well-refinèd pen.
Hearing you praised, I say, " 'Tis so, 'tis true,"
And to the most of praise add something more;
But that is in my thought, whose love to you,
Though words come hindmost, holds his rank before.
Then others for the breath of words respect,
Me for my dumb thoughts, speaking in effect.

86

Was it the proud full sail of his great verse,
Bound for the prize of all-too-precious you,
That did my ripe thoughts in my brain inhearse,
Making their tomb the womb wherein they grew?
Was it his spirit, by spirits taught to write
Above a mortal pitch, that struck me dead?
No, neither he, nor his compeers by night
Giving him aid, my verse astonishèd.
He, nor that affable-familiar ghost
Which nightly gulls him with intelligence,
As victors, of my silence cannot boast;
I was not sick of any fear from thence,
But when your countenance filled up his line,
Then lacked I matter; that enfeebled mine.

87

Farewell! thou art too dear for my possessing,
And like enough thou know'st thy estimate:
The charter of thy worth gives thee releasing;
My bonds in thee are all determinate.
For how do I hold thee but by thy granting?
And for that riches where is my deserving?
The cause of this fair gift in me is wanting,
And so my patent back again is swerving.
Thyself thou gav'st, thy own worth then not knowing,
Or me to whom thou gav'st, else mistaking;
So thy great gift, upon misprision growing,
Comes home again, on better judgment making.
    Thus have I had thee, as a dream doth flatter,
    In sleep a king, but waking no such matter.

88

When thou shalt be disposed to set me light,
And place my merit in the eye of scorn,
Upon thy side against myself I'll fight,
And prove thee virtuous, though thou art forsworn.
With mine own weakness being best acquainted,
Upon thy part I can set down a story
Of faults concealed, wherein I am attainted;
That thou, in losing me, shalt win much glory:
And I by this will be a gainer too;
For bending all my loving thoughts on thee,
The injuries that to myself I do,
Doing thee vantage, double-vantage me.
    Such is my love, to thee I so belong,
    That for thy right myself will bear all wrong.

89

Say that thou didst forsake me for some fault,
And I will comment upon that offense;
Speak of my lameness, and I straight will halt,
Against thy reasons making no defense.
Thou canst not, love, disgrace me half so ill,
To set a form upon desirèd change,
As I'll myself disgrace: knowing thy will,
I will acquaintance strangle, and look strange;
Be absent from thy walks; and in my tongue
Thy sweet-beloved name no more shall dwell,
Lest I, too much profane, should do it wrong,
And haply of our old acquaintance tell.
 For thee, against myself I'll vow debate,
 For I must ne'er love him whom thou dost hate.

90

Then hate me when thou wilt; if ever, now;
Now, while the world is bent my deeds to cross,
Join with the spite of Fortune, make me bow,
And do not drop in for an after-loss:
Ah, do not, when my heart hath scaped this sorrow,
Come in the rearward of a conquered woe!
Give not a windy night a rainy morrow,
To linger out a purposed overthrow.
If thou wilt leave me, do not leave me last,
When other petty griefs have done their spite,
But in the onset come; so shall I taste
At first the very worst of Fortune's might;
 And other strains of woe, which now seem woe,
 Compared with loss of thee will not seem so.

91

Some glory in their birth, some in their skill,
Some in their wealth, some in their body's force;
Some in their garments, though new-fangled ill;
Some in their hawks and hounds, some in their horse;
And every humor hath his adjunct pleasure,
Wherein it finds a joy above the rest:
But these particulars are not my measure;
All these I better in one general best.
Thy love is better than high birth to me,
Richer than wealth, prouder than garments' cost,
Of more delight than hawks or horses be;
And, having thee, of all men's pride I boast:
    Wretched in this alone, that thou mayst take
    All this away, and me most wretched make.

92

But do thy worst to steal thyself away,
For term of life thou art assurèd mine;
And life no longer than thy love will stay,
For it depends upon that love of thine.
Then need I not to fear the worst of wrongs,
When in the least of them my life hath end.
I see a better state to me belongs
Than that which on thy humor doth depend:
Thou canst not vex me with inconstant mind,
Since that my life on thy revolt doth lie.
O, what a happy title do I find,
Happy to have thy love, happy to die!
    But what's so blessèd-fair that fears no blot?—
    Thou mayst be false, and yet I know it not.

93

So shall I live, supposing thou art true,
Like a deceivèd husband; so love's face
May still seem love to me, though altered new;
Thy looks with me, thy heart in other place:
For there can live no hatred in thine eye,
Therefore in that I cannot know thy change.
In many's looks the false heart's history
Is writ, in moods and frowns and wrinkles strange,
But heaven in thy creation did decree
That in thy face sweet love should ever dwell;
Whate'er thy thoughts or thy heart's workings be,
Thy looks should nothing thence but sweetness tell.
    How like Eve's apple doth thy beauty grow,
    If thy sweet virtue answer not thy show!

94

They that have power to hurt and will do none,
That do not do the thing they most do show,
Who, moving others, are themselves as stone,
Unmovèd, cold, and to temptation slow;
They rightly do inherit heaven's graces,
And husband nature's riches from expense;
They are the lords and owners of their faces,
Others but stewards of their excellence.
The summer's flower is to the summer sweet,
Though to itself it only live and die;
But if that flower with base infection meet,
The basest weed outbraves his dignity:
    For sweetest things turn sourest by their deeds;
    Lilies that fester smell far worse than weeds.

95

How sweet and lovely dost thou make the shame
Which, like a canker in the fragrant rose,
Doth spot the beauty of thy budding name!
O, in what sweets dost thou thy sins enclose!
That tongue that tells the story of thy days,
Making lascivious comments on thy sport,;
Cannot dispraise but in a kind of praise;
Naming thy name blesses an ill report.
O, what a mansion have those vices got
Which for their habitation chose out thee,
Where beauty's veil doth cover every blot,
And all things turn to fair that eyes can see!
 Take heed, dear heart, of this large privilege;
 The hardest knife ill-used doth lose his edge.

96

Some say, thy fault is youth, some, wantonness;
Some say, thy grace is youth and gentle sport;
Both grace and faults are loved of more and less:
Thou mak'st faults graces that to thee resort.
As on the finger of a thronèd queen
The basest jewel will be well esteemed,
So are those errors that in thee are seen
To truths translated, and for true things deemed.
How many lambs might the stern wolf betray,
If like a lamb he could his looks translate!
How many gazers might'st thou lead away,
If thou wouldst use the strength of all thy state!
 But do not so; I love thee in such sort,
 As, thou being mine, mine is thy good report.

97

How like a winter hath my absence been
From thee, the pleasure of the fleeting year!
What freezings have I felt, what dark days seen!
What old December's bareness everywhere!
And yet this time removed was summer's time;
The teeming autumn, big with rich increase,
Bearing the wanton burden of the prime,
Like widowed wombs after their lords' decease:
Yet this abundant issue seemed to me
But hope of orphans and unfathered fruit;
For summer and his pleasures wait on thee,
And, thou away, the very birds are mute;
    Or, if they sing, 'tis with so dull a cheer,
    That leaves look pale, dreading the winter's near.

98

From you have I been absent in the spring,
When proud-pied April, dressed in all his trim,
Had put a spirit of youth in everything,
That heavy Saturn laughed and leaped with him.
Yet nor the lays of birds, nor the sweet smell
Of different flowers in odor and in hue,
Could make me any summer's story tell,
Or from their proud lap pluck them where they grew:
Nor did I wonder at the lily's white,
Nor praise the deep vermilion in the rose;
They were but sweet, but figures of delight,
Drawn after you—you pattern of all those.
    Yet seemed it winter still, and, you away,
    As with your shadow I with these did play.

99

The forward violet thus did I chide—
"Sweet thief, whence didst thou steal thy sweet that smells,
If not from my love's breath? The purple pride
Which on thy soft cheek for complexion dwells,
In my love's veins thou hast too grossly dyed."
The lily I condemned for thy hand,
And buds of marjoram had stolen thy hair:
The roses fearfully on thorns did stand,
One blushing shame, another white despair;
A third, nor red nor white, had stolen of both,
And to his robbery had annexed thy breath;
But, for his theft, in pride of all his growth
A vengeful canker eat him up to death.
    More flowers I noted, yet I none could see,
    But sweet or color it had stolen from thee.

Where art thou, Muse, that thou forgett'st so long
To speak of that which gives thee all thy might?
Spend'st thou thy fury on some worthless song,
Darkening thy power to lend base subjects light?
Return, forgetful Muse, and straight redeem
In gentle numbers time so idly spent;
Sing to the ear that doth thy lays esteem
And gives thy pen both skill and argument.
Rise, resty Muse, my love's sweet face survey,
If Time have any wrinkle graven there;
If any, be a satire to decay,
And make Time's spoils despisèd everywhere.
    Give my love fame faster than Time wastes life;
    So thou prevent'st his scythe and crookèd knife.

O, truant Muse, what shall be thy amends
For thy neglect of truth in beauty dyed?
Both truth and beauty on my love depends;
So dost thou too, and therein dignified.
Make answer, Muse: wilt thou not haply say,
"Truth needs no color with his color fixed;
Beauty no pencil, beauty's truth to lay;
But best is best, if never intermixed?"—
Because he needs no praise, wilt thou be dumb?
Excuse not silence so; for't lies in thee
To make him much outlive a gilded tomb,
And to be praised of ages yet to be.
    Then do thy office, Muse; I teach thee how
    To make him seem long hence as he shows now.

102

My love is strengthened, though more weak in seeming;
I love not less, though less the show appear;
That love is merchandized whose rich esteeming
The owner's tongue doth publish everywhere.
Our love was new, and then but in the spring,
When I was wont to greet it with my lays;
As Philomel in summer's front doth sing,
And stops her pipe in growth of riper days:
Not that the summer is less pleasant now
Than when her mournful hymns did hush the night,
But that wild music burdens every bough,
And sweets grown common lose their dear delight.
    Therefore, like her, I sometime hold my tongue,
    Because I would not dull you with my song.

103

Alack, what poverty my Muse brings forth,
That having such a scope to show her pride,
The argument, all bare, is of more worth
Than when it hath my added praise beside!
O, blame me not, if I no more can write!
Look in your glass, and there appears a face
That overgoes my blunt invention quite,
Dulling my lines, and doing me disgrace.
Were it not sinful, then, striving to mend,
To mar the subject that before was well?
For to no other pass my verses tend
Than of your graces and your gifts to tell;
    And more, much more, than in your verse can sit,
    Your own glass shows you when you look in it.

104

To me, fair friend, you never can be old,
For as you were when first your eye I eyed,
Such seems your beauty still. Three winters' cold
Have from the forests shook three summers' pride,
Three beauteous springs to yellow autumn turned
In process of the seasons have I seen,
Three April perfumes in three hot Junes burned,
Since first I saw you fresh, which yet are green.
Ah, yet doth beauty, like a dial hand,
Steal from his figure, and no pace perceived!
So your sweet hue, which methinks still doth stand,
Hath motion, and mine eye may be deceived:
    For fear of which, hear this, thou age unbred—
    Ere you were born was beauty's summer dead.

105

Let not my love be called idolatry,
Nor my belovèd as an idol show,
Since all alike my songs and praises be
To one, of one, still such, and ever so.
Kind is my love today, tomorrow kind,
Still constant in a wondrous excellence;
Therefore my verse to constancy confined,
One thing expressing, leaves out difference.
Fair, kind, and true, is all my argument—
Fair, kind, and true, varying to other words;
And in this change is my invention spent,
Three themes in one, which wondrous scope affords.
　　Fair, kind, and true, have often lived alone,
　　Which three till now never kept seat in one.

106

When in the chronicle of wasted time
I see descriptions of the fairest wights,
And beauty making beautiful old rhyme
In praise of ladies dead and lovely knights,
Then in the blazon of sweet beauty's best,
Of hand, of foot, of lip, of eye, of brow,
I see their antique pen would have expressed
Even such a beauty as you master now.
So all their praises are but prophecies
Of this our time, all you prefiguring;
And, for they looked but with divining eyes,
They had not skill enough your worth to sing:
　　For we, which now behold these present days,
　　Have eyes to wonder, but lack tongues to praise.

107

Not mine own fears, nor the prophetic soul
Of the wide world dreaming on things to come,
Can yet the lease of my true love control,
Supposed as forfeit to a confined doom.
The mortal moon hath her eclipse endured,
And the sad augurs mock their own presage;
Incertainties now crown themselves assured,
And peace proclaims olives of endless age.
Now with the drops of this most balmy time
My love looks fresh, and Death to me subscribes,
Since, spite of him, I'll live in this poor rhyme,
While he insults o'er dull and speechless tribes:
    And thou in this shalt find thy monument,
    When tyrants' crests and tombs of brass are spent.

108

What's in the brain, that ink may character,
Which hath not figured to thee my true spirit?
What's new to speak, what new to register,
That may express my love, or thy dear merit?
Nothing, sweet boy; but yet, like prayers divine,
I must each day say o'er the very same;
Counting no old thing old, thou mine, I thine,
Even as when first I hallowed thy fair name.
So that eternal love in love's fresh case
Weighs not the dust and injury of age,
Nor gives to necessary wrinkles place,
But makes antiquity for aye his page;
    Finding the first conceit of love there bred,
    Where time and outward form would show it dead.

O, never say that I was false of heart,
Though absence seemed my flame to qualify!
As easy might I from myself depart,
As from my soul, which in thy breast doth lie:
That is my home of love: if I have ranged,
Like him that travels, I return again;
Just to the time, not with the time exchanged—
So that myself bring water for my stain.
Never believe, though in my nature reigned
All frailties that besiege all kinds of blood,
That it could so preposterously be stained,
To leave for nothing all thy sum of good;
    For nothing this wide universe I call,
    Save thou, my rose; in it thou art my all.

Alas, 'tis true I have gone here and there,
And made myself a motley to the view,
Gored mine own thoughts, sold cheap what is most dear,
Made old offenses of affections new.
Most true it is that I have looked on truth
Askance and strangely; but, by all above,
These blenches gave my heart another youth,
And worse essays proved thee my best of love.
Now all is done, have what shall have no end:
Mine appetite I never more will grind
On newer proof, to try an older friend,
A god in love, to whom I am confined.
    Then give me welcome, next my heaven the best,
    Even to thy pure and most-most loving breast.

111

O, for my sake do you with Fortune chide,
The guilty goddess of my harmful deeds,
That did not better for my life provide,
Than public means, which public manners breeds.
Thence comes it that my name receives a brand;
And almost thence my nature is subdued
To what it works in, like the dyer's hand:
Pity me, then, and wish I were renewed;
Whilst, like a willing patient, I will drink
Potions of eisel 'gainst my strong infection;
No bitterness that I will bitter think,
Nor double penance, to correct correction.
    Pity me, then, dear friend, and I assure ye,
    Even that your pity is enough to cure me.

112

Your love and pity doth th'impression fill
Which vulgar scandal stamped upon my brow;
For what care I who calls me well or ill,
So you o'er-green my bad, my good allow?
You are my all-the-world, and I must strive
To know my shames and praises from your tongue;
None else to me, nor I to none alive,
That my steeled sense or changes right or wrong.
In so profound abysm I throw all care
Of others' voices, that my adder's sense
To critic and to flatterer stopped are.
Mark how with my neglect I do dispense—
    You are so strongly in my purpose bred,
    That all the world besides methinks are dead.

113

Since I left you, mine eye is in my mind;
And that which governs me to go about
Doth part his function, and is partly blind,
Seems seeing, but effectually is out;
For it no form delivers to the heart
Of bird, of flower, or shape, which it doth latch:
Of his quick objects hath the mind no part,
Nor his own vision holds what it doth catch;
For if it see the rud'st or gentlest sight
The most sweet favor or deformèd'st creature,
The mountain or the sea, the day or night,
The crow or dove, it shapes them to your feature:
    Incapable of more, replete with you,
    My most true mind thus mak'th mine untrue.

114

Or whether doth my mind, being crowned with you,
Drink up the monarch's plague, this flattery?
Or whether shall I say, mine eye saith true,
And that your love taught it this alchemy,
To make of monsters and things indigest
Such cherubins as your sweet self resemble,
Creating every bad a perfect best,
As fast as objects to his beams assemble?
O, 'tis the first; 'tis flattery in my seeing,
And my great mind most kingly drinks it up:
Mine eye well knows what with his gust is 'greeing,
And to his palate doth prepare the cup:
    If it be poison'd, 'tis the lesser sin
    That mine eye loves it, and doth first begin.

Those lines that I before have writ do lie;
Even those that said I could not love you dearer:
Yet then my judgment knew no reason why
My most full flame should afterwards burn clearer.
But reckoning Time, whose millioned accidents
Creep in 'twixt vows, and change decrees of kings,
Tan sacred beauty, blunt the sharp'st intents,
Divert strong minds to the course of altering things;
Alas, why, fearing of Time's tyranny,
Might I not then say, "Now I love you best,"
When I was certain o'er incertainty,
Crowning the present, doubting of the rest?
    Love is a babe; then might I not say so,
    To give full growth to that which still doth grow?

Let me not to the marriage of true minds
Admit impediments. Love is not love
Which alters when it alteration finds,
Or bends with the remover to remove:
O, no! it is an ever-fixèd mark,
That looks on tempests, and is never shaken;
It is the star to every wandering bark,
Whose worth's unknown, although his height be taken.
Love's not Time's fool, though rosy lips and cheeks
Within his bending sickle's compass come;
Love alters not with his brief hours and weeks,
But bears it out even to the edge of doom.
    If this be error, and upon me proved,
    I never writ, nor no man ever loved.

117

Accuse me thus—that I have scanted all
Wherein I should your great deserts repay;
Forgot upon your dearest love to call,
Whereto all bonds do tie me day by day;
That I have frequent been with unknown minds,
And given to time your own dear-purchased right;
That I have hoisted sail to all the winds
Which should transport me farthest from your sight.
Book both my willfulness and errors down,
And on just proof surmise accumulate;
Bring me within the level of your flown,
But shoot not at me in your wakened hate;
    Since my appeal says I did strive to prove
    The constancy and virtue of your love.

118

Like as, to make our appetites more keen,
With eager compounds we our palate urge;
As, to prevent our maladies unseen,
We sicken to shun sickness when we purge;
Even so, being full of your ne'er-cloying sweetness,
To bitter sauces did I frame my feeding;
And, sick of welfare, found a kind of meetness
To be diseased, ere that there was true needing.
Thus policy in love, t'anticipate
The ills that were not, grew to faults assured,
And brought to medicine a healthful state,
Which, rank of goodness, would by ill be cured.
    But thence I learn, and find the lesson true,
    Drugs poison him that so fell sick of you.

What potions have I drunk of siren tears,
Distilled from limbecks foul as hell within,
Applying fears to hopes, and hopes to fears,
Still losing when I saw myself to win!
What wretched errors hath my heart committed,
Whilst it hath thought itself so blessèd never!
How have mine eyes out of their spheres been fitted,
In the distraction of this madding fever!
O, benefit of ill! Now I find true
That better is by evil still made better;
And ruined love, when it is built anew,
Grows fairer than at first, more strong, far greater.
  So I return rebuked to my content,
  And gain by ill thrice more than I have spent.

That you were once unkind befriends me now,
And for that sorrow which I then did feel
Needs must I under my transgression bow,
Unless my nerves were brass or hammered steel.
For if you were by my unkindness shaken,
As I by yours, you've passed a hell of time;
And I, a tyrant, have no leisure taken
To weigh how once I suffered in your crime.
O, that our night of woe might have remembered
My deepest sense, how hard true sorrow hits,
And soon to you, as you to me then, tendered
The humble salve which wounded bosoms fits!
  But that your trespass now becomes a fee;
  Mine ransoms yours, and yours must ransom me.

'Tis better to be vile than vile esteemed,
When not to be receives reproach of being,
And the just pleasure lost, which is so deemed
Not by our feeling, but by others' seeing:
For why should others' false-adulterate eyes
Give salutation to my sportive blood?
Or on my frailties why are frailer spies,
Which in their wills count bad what I think good?
No—I am that I am; and they that level
At my abuses reckon up their own:
I may be straight, though they themselves be bevel;
By their rank thoughts my deeds must not be shown;
    Unless this general evil they maintain—
    All men are bad, and in their badness reign.

Thy gift, thy tables, are within my brain
Full charactered with lasting memory,
Which shall above that idle rank remain,
Beyond all date, even to eternity:
Or, at the least, so long as brain and heart
Have faculty by nature to subsist;
Till each to razed oblivion yield his part
Of thee, thy record never can be missed.
That poor retention could not so much hold,
Nor need I tallies thy dear love to score;
Therefore to give them from me was I bold,
To trust those tables that receive thee more:
    To keep an adjunct to remember thee,
    Were to import forgetfulness in me.

123

No, Time, thou shalt not boast that I do change!
Thy pyramids built up with newer might
To me are nothing novel, nothing strange;
They are but dressings of a former sight.
Our dates are brief, and therefore we admire
What thou dost foist upon us that is old;
And rather make them born to our desire
Than think that we before have heard them told.
Thy registers and thee I both defy,
Not wondering at the present nor the past;
For thy records and what we see do lie,
Made more or less by thy continual haste.
    This I do vow, and this shall ever be,
    I will be true, despite thy scythe and thee.

124

If my dear love were but the child of state,
It might for Fortune's bastard be unfathered,
As subject to Time's love or to Time's hate,
Weeds among weeds, or flowers with flowers gathered.
No, it was builded far from accident;
It suffers not in smiling pomp, nor falls
Under the blow of thrallèd discontent,
Whereto th'inviting time our fashion calls:
It fears not Policy, that heretic,
Which works on leases of short-numbered hours,
But all alone stands hugely politic,
That it nor grows with heat nor drowns with showers.
    To this I witness call the fools of Time,
    Which die for goodness, who have lived for crime.

125

Were't aught to me I bore the canopy,
With my extern the outward honoring,
Or laid great bases for eternity,
Which proves more short than waste or ruining?
Have I not seen dwellers on form and favor
Lose all, and more, by paying too much rent,
For compound sweet forgoing simple savor,
Pitiful thrivers, in their gazing spent?
No—let me be obsequious in thy heart,
And take thou my oblation, poor but free,
Which is not mixed with seconds, knows no art,
But mutual render, only me for thee.
　　　Hence, thou suborned informer! A true soul
　　　When most impeached stands least in thy control.

126

O thou, my lovely boy, who in thy power
Dost hold Time's fickle glass, his sickle hour;
Who hast by waning grown, and therein show'st
Thy lovers withering, as thy sweet self grow'st;
If Nature, sovereign mistress over wrack,
As thou goest onwards, still will pluck thee back,
She keeps thee to this purpose, that her skill
May Time disgrace, and wretched minutes kill.
Yet fear her, O thou minion of her pleasure!
She may detain, but not still keep, her treasure:
Her audit, though delayed, answered must be,
And her quietus is to render thee.

127

In the old age black was not counted fair,
Or if it were, it bore not beauty's name;
But now is black beauty's successive heir,
And beauty slandered with a bastard shame:
For since each hand hath put on nature's power,
Fairing the foul with art's false-borrowed face,
Sweet beauty hath no name, no holy bower,
But is profaned, if not lives in disgrace.
Therefore my mistress' eyes are raven black,
Her eyes so suited; and they mourners seem
At such who, not born fair, no beauty lack,
Sland'ring creation with a false esteem:
    Yet so they mourn, becoming of their woe,
    That every tongue says beauty should look so.

128

How oft, when thou, my music, music play'st,
Upon that blessèd wood whose motion sounds
With thy sweet fingers, when thou gently sway'st
The wiry concord that mine ear confounds,
Do I envy those jacks, that nimble leap
To kiss the tender inward of thy hand,
Whilst my poor lips, which should that harvest reap,
At the wood's boldness by thee blushing stand!
To be so tickled, they would change their state
And situation with those dancing chips,
O'er whom thy fingers walk with gentle gait,
Making dead wood more blest than living lips.
    Since saucy jacks so happy are in this,
    Give them thy fingers, me thy lips to kiss.

Th'expense of spirit in a waste of shame
Is lust in action; and till action, lust
Is perjured, murd'rous, bloody, full of blame.
Savage, extreme, rude, cruel, not to trust;
Enjoyed no sooner but despisèd straight;
Past reason hunted; and no sooner had,
Past reason hated, as a swallowed bait,
On purpose laid to make the taker mad:
Mad in pursuit, and in possession so;
Had, having, and in quest to have, extreme;
A bliss in proof—and proved, a very woe;
Before, a joy proposed; behind, a dream.
    All this the world well knows; yet none knows well
    To shun the heaven that leads men to this hell.

My mistress' eyes are nothing like the sun;
Coral is far more red than her lips' red:
If snow be white, why then her breasts are dun;
If hairs be wires, black wires grow on her head.
I have seen roses, damasked red and white,
But no such roses see I in her cheeks;
And in some perfumes is there more delight
Than in the breath that from my mistress reeks.
I love to hear her speak—yet well I know
That music hath a far more pleasing sound;
I grant I never saw a goddess go—
My mistress, when she walks, treads on the ground:
    And yet, by heaven, I think my love as rare
    As any she belied with false compare!

131

Thou art as tyrannous, so as thou art,
As those whose beauties proudly make them cruel;
For well thou know'st to my dear-doting heart
Thou art the fairest and most precious jewel.
Yet, in good faith, some say that thee behold,
Thy face hath not the power to make love groan:
To say they err, I dare not be so bold,
Although I swear it to myself alone.
And, to be sure that is not false I swear,
A thousand groans, but thinking on thy face,
One on another's neck, do witness bear
Thy black is fairest in my judgment's place.
    In nothing art thou black save in thy deeds,
    And thence this slander, as I think, proceeds.

132

Thine eyes I love, and they, as pitying me,
Knowing thy heart torment me with disdain,
Have put on black, and loving mourners be,
Looking with pretty ruth upon my pain.
And truly not the morning sun of heaven
Better becomes the gray cheeks of the east,
Nor that full star that ushers in the even
Doth half that glory to the sober west,
As those two mourning eyes become thy face:
O, let it then as well beseem thy heart
To mourn for me, since mourning doth thee grace,
And suit thy pity like in every part.
    Then will I swear beauty herself is black,
    And all they foul that thy complexion lack.

133

Beshrew that heart that makes my heart to groan
For that deep wound it gives my friend and me!
Is't not enough to torture me alone,
But slave to slavery my sweet'st friend must be?
Me from myself thy cruel eye hath taken,
And my next self thou harder hast engrossed:
Of him, myself, and thee, I am forsaken;
A torment thrice threefold thus to be crossed.
Prison my heart in thy steel bosom's ward,
But then my friend's heart let my poor heart bail;
Whoe'er keeps me, let my heart be his guard;
Thou canst not then use rigor in my jail:
    And yet thou wilt; for I, being pent in thee,
    Perforce am thine, and all that is in me.

134

So, now I have confessed that he is thine,
And I myself am mortgaged to thy will,
Myself I'll forfeit, so that other mine
Thou wilt restore, to be my comfort still:
But thou wilt not, nor he will not be free,
For thou art covetous, and he is kind;
He learned but, surety-like, to write for me,
Under that bond that him as fast doth bind.
The statue of thy beauty thou wilt take,
Thou usurer, that putt'st forth all to use,
And sue a friend came debtor for my sake;
So him I lose through my unkind abuse.
    Him have I lost; thou hast both him and me:
    He pays the whole, and yet am I not free.

135

Whoever hath her wish, thou hast thy *Will*,
And *Will* to boot, and *Will* in overplus;
More than enough am I that vex thee still,
To thy sweet will making addition thus.
Wilt thou, whose will is large and spacious,
Not once vouchsafe to hide my will in thine?
Shall will in others seem right gracious,
And in my will no fair acceptance shine?
The sea, all water, yet receives rain still,
And, in abundance, addeth to his store;
So thou, being rich in *Will*, add to thy *Will*
One will of mine, to make thy large *Will* more.
    Let no unkind, no fair beseechers kill;
    Think all but one, and me in that one *Will*.

136

If thy soul check thee that I come so near,
Swear to thy blind soul that I was thy *Will*,
And will, thy soul knows, is admitted there;
Thus far for love, my love-suit, sweet, fulfill.
Will will fulfill the treasure of thy love,
Ay, fill it full with wills, and my will one,
In things of great receipt with ease we prove
Among a number one is reckoned none:
Then in the number let me pass untold,
Though in thy store's account I one must be;
For nothing hold me, so it please thee hold
That nothing me, a something sweet to thee:
    Make but my name thy love, and love that still,
    And then thou lov'st me—for my name is *Will*.

137

Thou blind fool, Love, what dost thou to mine eyes,
That they behold, and see not what they see?
They know what beauty is, see where it lies,
Yet what the best is, take the worst to be.
If eyes, corrupt by over-partial looks,
Be anchored in the bay where all men ride,
Why of eyes' falsehood hast thou forgèd hooks,
Whereto the judgment of my heart is tied?
Why should my heart think that a several plot
Which my heart knows the wide world's common place?
Or mine eyes, seeing this, say this is not,
To put fair truth upon so foul a face?
    In things right-true my heart and eyes have erred,
    And to this false plague are they now transferred.

138

When my love swears that she is made of truth
I do believe her, though I know she lies,
That she might think me some untutored youth,
Unlearnèd in the world's false subtleties.
Thus vainly thinking that she thinks me young,
Although she knows my days are past the best,
Simply I credit her false-speaking tongue:
On both sides thus is simple truth suppressed.
But wherefore says she not she is unjust?
And wherefore say not I that I am old?
O, love's best habit is in seeming trust,
And age in love loves not to have years told:
    Therefore I lie with her and she with me,
    And in our faults by lies we flattered be.

O, call not me to justify the wrong
That thy unkindness lays upon my heart;
Wound me not with thine eye, but with thy tongue;
Use power with power, and slay me not by art.
Tell me thou lov'st elsewhere; but in my sight,
Dear heart, forbear to glance thine eye aside:
What need'st thou wound with cunning, when thy might
Is more than my o'erpressed defense can bide?
Let me excuse thee: ah, my love well knows
Her pretty looks have been mine enemies!
And therefore from my face she turns my foes,
That they elsewhere might dart their injuries:
    Yet do not so; but since I am near slain,
    Kill me outright with looks, and rid my pain.

140

Be wise as thou art cruel; do not press
My tongue-tied patience with too much disdain;
Lest sorrow lend me words, and words express
The manner of my pity-wanting pain.
If I might teach thee wit, better it were,
Though not to love, yet, love, to tell me so—
As testy sick men, when their deaths be near,
No news but health from their physicians know—
For, if I should despair, I should grow mad,
And in my madness might speak ill of thee:
Now this ill-wresting world is grown so bad,
Mad slanderers by mad ears believèd be.
    That I may not be so, nor thou belied,
    Bear thine eyes straight, though thy proud heart
        go wide.

In faith, I do not love thee with mine eyes,
For they in thee a thousand errors note;
But 'tis my heart that loves what they despise,
Who, in despite of view, is pleased to dote;
Nor are mine ears with thy tongue's tune delighted;
Nor tender feeling, to base touches prone,
Nor taste, nor smell, desire to be invited
To any sensual feast with thee alone:
But my five wits nor my five senses can
Dissuade one foolish heart from serving thee,
Who leaves unswayed the likeness of a man,
Thy proud heart's slave and vassal wretch to be:
    Only my plague thus far I count my gain,
    That she that makes me sin awards me pain.

142

Love is my sin, and thy dear virtue hate,
Hate of my sin, grounded on sinful loving:
O, but with mine compare thou thine own state,
And thou shalt find it merits not reproving;
Or, if it do, not from those lips of thine,
That have profaned their scarlet ornaments,
And sealed false bonds of love as oft as mine;
Robbed others' beds' revenues of their rents.
Be it lawful I love thee, as thou lov'st those
Whom thine eyes woo as mine importune thee:
Root pity in thy heart, that, when it grows,
Thy pity may deserve to pitied be.
    If thou dost seek to have what thou dost hide,
    By self-example mayst thou be denied!

Lo, as a careful housewife runs to catch
One of her feathered creatures broke away,
Sets down her babe, and makes all swift dispatch
In pursuit of the thing she would have stay;
Whilst her neglected child holds her in chase,
Cries to catch her whose busy care is bent
To follow that which flies before her face,
Not prizing her poor infant's discontent;
So runn'st thou after that which flies from thee,
Whilst I thy babe chase thee afar behind;
But if thou catch thy hope, turn back to me,
And play the mother's part, kiss me, be kind:
    So will I pray that thou mayst have thy *Will*,
    If thou turn back, and my loud crying still.

Two loves I have of comfort and despair,
Which like two spirits do suggest me still;
The better angel is a man right fair,
The worser spirit a woman colored ill.
To win me soon to hell, my female evil
Tempteth my better angel from my side,
And would corrupt my saint to be a devil,
Wooing his purity with her foul pride.
And whether that my angel be turned fiend,
Suspect I may, yet not directly tell;
But being both from me, both to each friend,
I guess one angel in another's hell:
    Yet this shall I ne'er know, but live in doubt,
    Till my bad angel fire my good one out.

145

Those lips that Love's own hand did make
Breathed forth the sound that said, "I hate,"
To me that languished for her sake:
But when she saw my woeful state,
Straight in her heart did mercy come,
Chiding that tongue, that ever sweet
Was used in giving gentle doom;
And taught it thus anew to greet;
"I hate," she altered with an end,
That followed it as gentle day
Doth follow night, who, like a fiend,
From heaven to hell is flown away;
    "I hate," from hate away she threw,
    And saved my life, saying—"not you."

146

Poor soul, the center of my sinful earth,
Fooled by these rebel powers that thee array,
Why dost thou pine within and suffer dearth,
Painting thy outward walls so costly gay?
Why so large cost, having so short a lease,
Dost thou upon thy fading mansion spend?
Shall worms, inheritors of this excess,
Eat up thy charge? Is this thy body's end?
Then, soul, live thou upon thy servant's loss,
And let that pine to aggravate thy store;
Buy terms divine in selling hours of dross;
Within be fed, without be rich no more:
    So shalt thou feed on Death, that feeds on men,
    And Death once dead, there's no more dying then.

My love is as a fever, longing still
For that which longer nurseth the disease;
Feeding on that which doth preserve the ill,
Th'uncertain sickly appetite to please.
My reason, the physician to my love,
Angry that his prescriptions are not kept,
Hath left me, and I, desperate now, approve
Desire is death, which physic did except.
Past cure I am, now reason is past care,
And frantic-mad with evermore unrest;
My thoughts and my discourse as madmen's are,
At random from the truth vainly expressed;
    For I have sworn thee fair, and thought thee bright,
    Who art as black as hell, as dark as night.

O me, what eyes hath Love put in my head,
Which have no correspondence with true sight!
Or, if they have, where is my judgment fled,
That censures falsely what they see aright?
If that be fair whereon my false eyes dote,
What means the world to say it is not so?
If it be not, then love doth well denote
Love's eye is not so true as all men's: no;
How can it? O, how can Love's eye be true,
That is so vexed with watching and with tears?
No marvel, then, though I mistake my view;
The sun itself sees not, till heaven clears.
    O, cunning love! with tears thou keep'st me blind,
    Lest eyes well-seeing thy foul faults should find.

149

Canst thou, O cruel, say I love thee not,
When I, against myself, with thee partake?
Do I not think on thee, when I forgot
Am of myself, all tyrant, for thy sake?
Who hateth thee that I do call my friend?
On whom frown'st thou that I do fawn upon?
Nay if thou lour'st on me, do I not spend
Revenge upon myself with present moan?
What merit do I in myself respect,
That is so proud thy service to despise,
When all my best doth worship thy defect,
Commanded by the motion of thine eyes?
  But, love, hate on, for now I know thy mind;
  Those that can see thou lov'st, and I am blind.

150

O, from what power hast thou this powerful might,
With insufficiency my heart to sway?
To make me give the lie to my true sight,
And swear that brightness doth not grace the day?
Whence hast thou this becoming of things ill,
That in the very refuse of thy deeds
There is such strength and warrantise of skill,
That, in my mind, thy worst all best exceeds?
Who taught thee how to make me love thee more,
The more I hear and see just cause of hate?
O, though I love what others do abhor,
With others thou shouldst not abhor my state:
  If thy unworthiness raised love in me,
  More worthy I to be beloved of thee.

151

Love is too young to know what conscience is;
Yet who knows not, conscience is born of love?
Then, gentle cheater, urge not my amiss,
Lest guilty of my faults thy sweet self prove:
For thou betraying me, I do betray
My nobler part to my gross body's treason;
My soul doth tell my body that he may
Triumph in love; flesh stays no farther reason;
But, rising,at thy name, doth point out thee
As his triumphant prize. Proud of this pride,
He is contented thy poor drudge to be,
To stand in thy affairs, fall by thy side.
   No want of conscience hold it that I call
   Her "love" for whose dear love I rise and fall.

152

In loving thee thou know'st I am forsworn,
But thou art twice forsworn, to me love swearing;
In act thy bed-vow broke, and new faith torn,
In vowing new hate after new love bearing.
But why of two oaths' breach do I accuse thee,
When I break twenty? I am perjured most;
For all my vows are oaths but to misuse thee,
And all my honest faith in thee is lost:
For I have sworn deep oaths of thy deep kindness,
Oaths of thy love, thy truth, thy constancy;
And, to enlighten thee, gave eyes to blindness,
Or made them swear against the thing they see;
   For I have sworn thee fair—more perjured eye,
   To swear, against the truth, so foul a lie!

153

Cupid laid by his brand, and fell asleep:
A maid of Dian's this advantage found,
And his love-kindling fire did quickly steep
In a cold valley-fountain of that ground;
Which borrowed from this holy fire of Love
A dateless-lively heat, still to endure,
And grew a seething bath, which yet men prove
Against strange maladies a sovereign cure.
But at my mistress' eye Love s brand new-fired,
The boy for trial needs would touch my breast;
I, sick withal, the help of bath desired,
And thither hied, a sad distempered guest,
    But found no cure: the bath for my help lies
    Where Cupid got new fire—my mistress' eyes.

154

The little Love-god, lying once asleep,
Laid by his side his heart-inflaming brand,
Whilst many nymphs that vowed chaste life to keep
Came tripping by; but in her maiden hand
The fairest votary took up that fire
Which many legions of true hearts had warmed;
And so the general of hot desire
Was sleeping by a virgin hand disarmed.
This brand she quenchèd in a cool well by,
Which from Love's fire took heat perpetual,
Growing a bath and healthful remedy
For men diseased; but I, my mistress' thrall,
    Came there for cure, and this by that I prove,
    Love's fire heats water, water cools not love.

A Lover's Complaint

A LOVER'S COMPLAINT

From off a hill whose concave womb re-worded
A plaintful story from a sist'ring vale,
My spirits t'attend this double voice accorded,
And down I laid to list the sad-tuned tale:
Ere long espied a fickle maid full pale,
Tearing of papers, breaking rings a-twain,
Storming her world with sorrow's wind and rain.

Upon her head a plaited hive of straw,
Which fortified her visage from the sun,
Whereon the thought might think sometime it saw
The carcass of a beauty spent and done:
Time had not scythèd all that youth begun,
Nor youth all quit; but, spite of heaven's fell rage,
Some beauty peeped through lattice of seared age.

Oft did she heave her napkin to her eyne,
Which on it had conceited characters,
Laund'ring the silken figures in the brine
That seasoned woe had pelleted in tears,
And often reading what contents it bears;
As often shrieking undistinguished woe,
In clamors of all size, both high and low.

Sometimes her leveled eyes their carriage ride,
As they did batt'ry to the spheres intend;
Sometime diverted their poor balls are tied
To th'orbèd earth; sometimes they do extend
Their view right on; anon their gazes lend
To every place at once, and, nowhere fixed,
The mind and sight distractedly commixed.

Her hair, nor loose nor tied in formal plat,
Proclaimed in her a careless hand of pride;
For some, untucked, descended her sheaved hat,
Hanging her pale and pinèd cheek beside;
Some in her threaden fillet still did bide,
And, true to bondage, would not break from thence,
Though slackly braided in loose negligence.

A thousand favors from a maund she drew
Of amber, crystal, and of beaded jet,
Which one by one she in a river threw,
Upon whose weeping margent she was set;
Like usury, applying wet to wet,
Or monarch's hands, that let not bounty fall
Where want cries some, but where excess begs all.

Of folded schedules had she many a one,
Which she perused, sighed, tore, and gave the flood;
Cracked many a ring of posied gold and bone,
Bidding them find their sepulchers in mud;
Found yet more letters sadly penned in blood,
With sleided silk feat and affectedly
Enswathed, and sealed to curious secrecy.

These often bathed she in her fluxive eyes,
And often kissed, and often 'gan to tear;
Cried, "O false blood, thou register of lies,
What unapprovèd witness dost thou bear!
Ink would have seemed more black and damnèd
    here!"
This said, in top of rage the lines she rents,
Big discontent so breaking their contents.

A reverend man that grazed his cattle nigh—
Sometime a blusterer, that the ruffle knew

Of court, of city, and had let go by
The swiftest hours, observèd as they flew—
Towards this afflicted fancy fastly drew;
And, privileged by age, desires to know
In brief the grounds and motives of her woe.

So slides he down upon his grainèd bat,
And comely-distant sits he by her side;
When he again desires her, being sat,
Her grievance with his hearing to divide:
If that from him there may be aught applied
Which may her suffering ecstasy assuage,
"Tis promised in the charity of age.

"Father," she says, "though in me you behold
The injury of many a blasting hour,
Let it not tell your judgment I am old;
Not age, but sorrow, over me hath power:
I might as yet have been a spreading flower,
Fresh to myself, if I had self-applied
Love to myself, and to no love beside.

"But, woe is me! Too early I attended
A youthful suit (it was to gain my grace)
O, one by nature's outwards so commended,
That maidens' eyes stuck over all his face:
Love lacked a dwelling, and made him her place;
And when in his fair parts she did abide,
She was new lodged, and newly deified.

"His browny locks did hang in crookèd curls;
And every light occasion of the wind
Upon his lips their silken parcels hurls.
What's sweet to do, to do will aptly find:

Each eye that saw him did enchant the mind;
For on his visage was in little drawn,
What largeness thinks in paradise was sawn.

"Small show of man was yet upon his chin;
His phoenix down began but to appear,
Like unshorn velvet, on that termless skin,
Whose bare outbragged the web it seemed to wear;
Yet showed his visage by that cost more dear;
And nice affections wavering stood in doubt
If best were as it was, or best without.

"His qualities were beauteous as his form,
For maiden-tongued he was, and thereof free;
Yet, if men moved him, was he such a storm
As oft 'twixt May and April is to see,
When winds breathe sweet, unruly though they be.
His rudeness so with his authorized youth
Did livery falseness in a pride of truth.

"Well could he ride, and often men would say
'That horse his mettle from his rider takes:
Proud of subjection, noble by the sway,
What rounds, what bounds, what course, what stop he
        makes!'
And controversy hence a question takes,
Whether the horse by him became his deed,
Or he his manage by the well-doing steed.

"But quickly on this side the verdict went;
His real habitude gave life and grace
To appertainings and to ornament,
Accomplished in himself, not in his case:
All aids, themselves made fairer by their place,
Came for additions; yet their purposed trim
Pieced not his grace, but were all graced by him.

"So on the tip of his subduing tongue
All kind of arguments and question deep.
All replication prompt, and reason strong,
For his advantage still did wake and sleep:
To make the weeper laugh, the laugher weep,
He had the dialect and different skill,
Catching all passions in his craft of will:

"That he did in the general bosom reign
Of young, of old; and sexes both enchanted
To dwell with him in thoughts, or to remain
In personal duty, following where he haunted:
Consents bewitched, ere he desire, have granted;
And daylight for him what he would say,
Asked their own wills, and made their wills obey.

"Many there were that did his picture get,
To serve their eyes, and in it put their mind;
Like fools that in th'imagination set
The goodly objects which abroad they find
Of lands and mansions, theirs in thought assigned;
And laboring in more pleasures to bestow them
Than the true gouty landlord which doth owe them:

"So many have, that never touched his hand,
Sweetly supposed them mistress of his heart.
My woeful self, that did in freedom stand,
And was my own fee-simple, (not in part)
What with his art in youth, and youth in art,
Threw my affections in his charmèd power,
Reserved the stalk, and gave him all my flower.

"Yet did I not, as some my equals did,
Demand of him, nor being desirèd yielded;
Finding myself in honor so forbid,

With safest distance I mine honor shielded:
Experience for me many bulwarks builded
Of proofs new-bleeding, which remained the foil
Of this false jewel, and his amorous spoil.

"But, ah, who ever shunned by precedent
The destined ill she must herself assay?
Or forced examples, 'gainst her own content,
To put the bypassed perils in her way?
Counsel may stop a while what will not stay;
For when we rage, advice is often seen
By blunting us to make our wits more keen.

"Nor gives it satisfaction to our blood,
That we must curb it upon others' proof;
To be forbod the sweets that seem so good,
For fear of harms that preach in our behoof.
O appetite, from judgment stand aloof!
The one a palate hath that needs will taste,
Though reason weep, and cry, 'It is thy last.'

"For further I could say this man's untrue,
And knew the patterns of his foul beguiling;
Heard where his plants in others' orchards grew,
Saw how deceits were gilded in his smiling;
Knew vows were ever brokers to defiling;
Thought characters and words merely but art,
And bastards of his foul adulterate heart.

"And long upon these terms I held my city,
Till thus he 'gan besiege me: 'Gentle maid,
Have of my suffering youth some feeling pity,
And be not of my holy vows afraid:
That's to ye sworn, to none was ever said;

For feasts of love I have been called unto,
Till now did ne'er invite, nor never vow.

" 'All my offenses that abroad you see
Are errors of the blood, none of the mind;
Love made them not; with acture they may be,
Where neither party is nor true nor kind:
They sought their shame that so their shame did find;
And so much less of shame in me remains,
By how much of me their reproach contains.

" 'Among the many that mine eyes have seen,
Not one whose flame my heart so much as warmèd,
Or my affection put to the smallest teen,
Or any of my leisures ever charmèd:
Harm have I done to them, but ne'er was harmèd;
Kept hearts in liveries, but mine own was free,
And reigned, commanding in his monarchy.

" 'Look here what tributes wounded fancies sent me,
Of paled pearls, and rubies red as blood;
Figuring that they their passions likewise lent me
Of grief and blushes, aptly understood
In bloodless white and the encrimsoned mood;
Effects of terror and dear modesty,
Encamped in hearts, but fighting outwardly.

" 'And, lo, behold these talents of their hair,
With twisted metal amorously impleached,
I have received from many a several fair—
Their kind acceptance weepingly beseeched,
With the annexions of fair gems enriched,
And deep-brained sonnets that did amplify
Each stone's dear nature, worth, and quality.

" 'The diamond?—why, 'twas beautiful and hard,
Whereto his invised properties did tend;
The deep-green em'rald, in whose fresh regard
Weak sights their sickly radiance do amend;
The heaven-hued sapphire and the opal blend
With objects manifold; each several stone,
With wit well blazoned, smiled or made some moan.

" 'Lo, all these trophies of affections hot,
Of pensived and subdued desires the tender,
Nature hath charged me that I hoard them not,
But yield them up where I myself must render,
That is, to you, my origin and ender;
For these, of force, must your oblations be,
Since I their altar, you enpatron me.

" 'O, then, advance of yours that phraseless hand,
Whose white weighs down the airy scale of praise;
Take all these similes to your own command,
Hallow'd with sighs that burning lungs did raise;
What me your minister, for you obeys,
Works under you; and to your audit comes
Their distract parcels in combinèd sums.

" 'Lo, this device was sent me from a nun,
Or sister sanctified, of holiest note;
Which late her noble suit in court did shun,
Whose rarest havings made the blossoms dote;
For she was sought by spirits of richest coat,
But kept cold distance, and did thence remove,
To spend her living in eternal love.

" 'But, O, my sweet, what labor is't to leave
The thing we have not, mast'ring what not strives—

Paling the place which did no form receive,
Playing patient sports in unconstrainèd gyves!
She that her fame so to herself contrives,
The scars of battle 'scapeth by the flight,
And makes her absence valiant, not her might.

" 'O, pardon me, in that my boast is true;
The accident which brought me to her eye,
Upon the moment did her force subdue,
And now she would the cagèd cloister fly:
Religious love put out religion's eye;
Not to be tempted, would she be immured,
And now, to tempt all, liberty procured.

" 'How mighty then you are, O, hear me tell!
The broken bosoms that to me belong
Have emptied their fountains in my well,
And mine I pour your ocean all among:
I strong o'er them, and you o'er me being strong,
Must for your victory us all congest,
As compound love to physic your cold breast.

" 'My parts had power to charm a sacred nun,
Who, disciplined, ay, dieted in grace,
Believed her eyes when they t'assail begun,
All vows and consecrations giving place.
O, most potential love! Vow, bond, nor space,
In thee hath neither sting, knot, nor confine,
For thou art all, and all things else are thine.

" 'When thou impressest, what are precepts worth
Of stale example? When thou wilt inflame,
How coldly these impediments stand forth
Of wealth, of filial fear, law, kindred, fame!

Love's arms are peace, 'gainst rule, 'gainst sense,
   'gainst shame,
And sweetens, in the suffering pangs it bears,
The aloes of all forces, shocks, and fears.

" 'Now all these hearts that do on mine depend,
Feeling it break, with bleeding groans they pine,
And supplicant their sighs to you extend,
To leave the batt'ry that you make 'gainst mine,
Lending soft audience to my sweet design,
And credent soul to that strong-bonded oath,
That shall prefer and undertake my troth.'

"This said, his wat'ry eyes he did dismount
Whose sights till then were leveled on my face;
Each cheek a river running from a fount
With brinish current downward flowed apace:
O, how the channel to the stream gave grace!
Who glazed with crystal gate the glowing roses
That flame through water which their hue encloses.

"O, father, what a hell of witchcraft lies
In the small orb of one particular tear!
But with the inundation of the eyes
What rocky heart to water will not wear?
What breast so cold that it is not warmèd here?
O cleft effect! Cold modesty, hot wrath,
Both fire from hence and chill extincture hath!

"For, lo, his passion, but an art of craft,
Even there resolved my reason into tears;
There my white stole of chastity I daffed,
Shook off my sober guards and civil fears;
Appear to him, as he to me appears,
All melting, though our drops this difference bore,
His poisoned me, and mine did him restore.

"In him a plenitude of subtle matter,
Applied to cautels, all strange forms receives,
Of burning blushes, of weeping water,
Or swooning paleness; and he takes and leaves,
In either's aptness, as it best deceives,
To blush at speeches rank, to weep at woes,
Or to turn white and swoon at tragic shows;

"That not a heart which in his level came
Could scape the hail of his all-hurting aim,
Showing fair nature is both kind and tame;
And, veiled in them, did win whom he would maim:
Against the thing he sought he would exclaim;
When he most burned in heart-wished luxury,
He preached pure maid, and praised cold chastity.

"Thus merely with the garment of a grace
The naked and concealèd fiend he covered,
That th'unexperient gave the tempter place,
Which, like a cherubin, above them hovered.
Who, young and simple, would not be so lovered?
Ah me! I fell; and yet do question make
What I should do again for such a sake.

"O, that infected moisture of his eye,
O, that false fire which in his cheek so glowed,
O, that forced thunder from his heart did fly,
O, that sad breath his spongy lungs bestowed,
O, all that borrowed motion, seeming owed,
Would yet again betray the fore-betrayed,
And new pervert a reconcilèd maid!"

Poems From
The Passionate
Pilgrim

Poems from
THE PASSIONATE PILGRIM

3

Did not the heavenly rhetoric of thine eye,
'Gainst whom the world could not hold argument,
Persuade my heart to his false perjury?
Vows for thee broke deserve not punishment.
A woman I foreswore; but, I will prove,
Thou being a goddess, I forswore not thee:
My vow was earthly, thou a heavenly love;
Thy grave being gained cures all disgrace in me.
My vow was breath, and breath a vapor is;
Then, thou fair sun, that on this earth doth shine,
Exhale this vapor vow; in thee it is:
If broken then, it is no fault of mine.
    If by me broke, what fool is not so wise
    To lose an oath to win a paradise?

4

Sweet Cytherea, sitting by a brook,
With young Adonis, lovely-fresh and green,
Did court the lad with many a lovely look—
Such looks as none could look but beauty's queen.
She told him stories to delight his ear;
She showed him favors to allure his eye;
To win his heart, she touched him here and there—
Touches so soft still conquer chastity—
But whether unripe years did want conceit,
Or he refused to take her figured proffer,
The tender nibbler would not touch the bait,

But smile and jest at every gentle offer:
  Then fell she on her back, fair queen and toward;
  He ran and ran away—ah, fool too froward!

5

If love make me forsworn, how shall I swear to love?
O, never faith could hold, if not to beauty vowed!
Though to myself forsworn, to thee I'll constant prove;
Those thoughts to me like oaks, to thee like osiers bowed.
Study his bias leaves, and makes his book thine eyes,
Where all those pleasures live that art can comprehend.
If knowledge be the mark, to know thee shall suffice;
Well learned is that tongue that well can thee commend;
All ignorant that soul that sees thee without wonder;
Which is to me some praise, that I thy parts admire:
Thine eye Jove's lightning seems, thy voice his dreadful thunder,
Which, not to anger bent, is music and sweet fire.
  Celestial as thou art, O, do not love that wrong,
  To sing the heavens' praise with such an earthly tongue!

6

Scarce had the sun dried up the dewy morn,
And scarce the herd gone to the hedge for shade,
When Cytherea, all in love forlorn,
A longing tarriance for Adonis made
Under an osier growing by a brook,
A brook where Adon used to cool his spleen:
Hot was the day; she hotter than did look
For his approach, that often there had been.
Anon he comes, and throws his mantle by,
And stood stark naked on the brook's green brim:
The sun looked on the world with glorious eye,

Yet not so wistly as this queen on him:
    He, spying her, bounced in, whereas he stood;
    "O Jove," quoth she, "why was not I a flood!"

7

Fair is my love, but not so fair as fickle;
Mild as a dove, but neither true nor trusty;
Brighter than glass, and yet, as glass is, brittle,
Softer than wax, and yet, as iron, rusty;
    A lily pale, with damask dye to grace her,
    None fairer, nor none falser to deface her.

Her lips to mine how often hath she joined,
Between each kiss her oaths of true love swearing!
How many tales to please me hath she coined,
Dreading my love, the loss thereof still fearing!
    Yet in the midst of all her pure protestings,
    Her faith, her oaths, her tears, and all were jestings.

She burnt with love, as straw with fire flameth,
She burnt out love, as soon as straw out-burneth;
She framed the love, and yet she foiled the framing,
She bade love last, and yet she fell a-turning.
    Was this a lover, or a lecher whether?
    Bad in the best, though excellent in neither.

9

Fair was the morn, when the fair queen of love,
[   ]
Paler for sorrow than her milk-white dove,
For Adon's sake, a youngster proud and wild;
Her stand she takes upon a steep-up hill:

Anon Adonis comes with horn and hounds;
She, seely queen, with more than love's good will,
Forbade the boy he should not pass those grounds;
"Once," quoth she, "did I see a fair sweet youth
Here in these brakes deep-wounded with a boar,
Deep in the thigh, a spectacle of ruth!
See in my thigh," quoth she, "here was the sore":
She showèd hers; he saw more wounds than one,
And blushing fled, and left her all alone.

10

Sweet rose, fair flower, untimely plucked, soon faded,
Plucked in the bud, and faded in the spring!
Bright orient pearl, alack! too timely shaded!
Fair creature, killed too soon by death's sharp sting!
Like a green plum that hangs upon a tree,
And falls, through wind, before the fall should be.

I weep for thee, and yet no cause I have;
For why thou left'st me nothing in thy will:
And yet thou left'st me more than I did crave;
For why I cravèd nothing of thee still:
O yes, dear friend, I pardon crave of thee—
Thy discontent thou didst bequeath to me.

12

Crabbèd age and youth cannot live together:
Youth is full of pleasance, age is full of care;
Youth like summer morn, age like winter weather;
Youth like summer brave, age like winter bare.
Youth is full of sport, age's breath is short;
Youth is nimble, age is lame;

Youth is hot and bold, age is weak and cold;
Youth is wild, and age is tame.
Age, I do abhor thee, youth, I do adore thee;
O, my love, my love is young!
Age, I do defy thee—O, sweet shepherd, hie thee!
For methinks thou stay'st too long.

13

Beauty is but a vain and doubtful good,
A shining gloss that fadeth suddenly;
A flower that dies when first it 'gins to bud;
A brittle glass that's broken presently:
A doubtful good, a gloss, a glass, a flower,
Lost, faded, broken, dead within an hour!

And as goods lost are seld or never found,
As faded gloss no rubbing will refresh,
As flowers dead lie withered on the ground,
As broken glass no cement can redress—
So beauty blemished once for ever's lost,
In spite of physic, painting, pain, and cost.

14

"Good night, good rest." Ah, neither be my share!
She bade good night, that kept my rest away;
And daffed me to a cabin hanged with care,
To descant on the doubts of my decay.
"Farewell," quoth she, "and come again tomorrow";
Fare well I could not, for I supped with sorrow.

Yet at my parting sweetly did she smile,
In scorn or friendship, nill I construe whether:

'Tmay be, she joyed to jest at my exile,
'Tmay be, again to make me wander thither:
   "Wander"—a word for shadows like myself,
   As take the pain, but cannot pluck the pelf.

Lord, how mine eyes throw gazes to the east!
My heart doth charge the watch; the morning rise
Doth cite each moving sense from idle rest.
Not daring trust the office of mine eyes,
   While Philomela sits and sings, I sit and mark,
   And wish her lays were tunèd like the lark;

For she doth welcome daylight with her ditty,
And daylight drives away dark dreaming night:
The night so packed, I post unto my pretty;
Heart hath his hope, and eyes their wishèd sight;
   Sorrow changed to solace, solace mixed with sorrow;
   For why she sighed, and bade me come tomorrow.

Were I with her, the night would post too soon;
But now are minutes added to the hours;
To spite me now, each minute seems a moon;
Yet not for me, shine sun to succor flowers!
   Pack night, peep day; good day, of night now borrow;
   Short, night, tonight, and length thyself tomorrow.

SONNETS TO SUNDRY
NOTES OF MUSIC

15

It was a lording's daughter, the fairest one of three,
That likèd of her master as well as well might be,
Till looking on an Englishman, the fair'st that eye could see,
   Her fancy fell a-turning.

Long was the combat doubtful that love with love did fight,
To leave the master loveless, or kill the gallant knight:
To put in practice either, alas, it was a spite
    Unto the silly damsel!

But one must be refusèd; more mickle was the pain,
That nothing could be usèd to turn them both to gain,
For of the two the trusty knight was wounded with disdain:
    Alas, she could not help it!

Thus art, with arms contending, was victor of the day,
Which by a gift of learning did bear the maid away:
Then, lullaby, the learned man hath got the lady gay;
    For now my song is ended.

16

On a day (alack the day!),
Love, whose month was ever May,
Spied a blossom passing fair,
Playing in the wanton air:
Through the velvet leaves the wind,
All unseen, 'gan passage find;
That the lover, sick to death,
Wished himself the heaven's breath.
"Air," quoth he, "thy cheeks may blow;
Air, would I might triumph so!
But, alas, my hand hath sworn
Ne'er to pluck thee from thy thorn!
Vow, alack, for youth unmeet,
Youth so apt to pluck a sweet.
Thou for whom Jove would swear
Juno but an Ethiope were;
And deny himself for Jove,
Turning mortal for thy love."

17

My flocks feed not, my ewes breed not,
My rams speed not, all is amiss:
Love is dying, faith's defying,
Heart's denying causer of this.
All my merry jigs are quite forgot—
All my lady's love is lost, God wot:
Where her faith was firmly fixed in love,
There a nay is placed without remove.
One seely cross wrought all my loss;
O, frowning Fortune, cursèd, fickle dame!
For now I see, inconstancy
More in women than in men remain.

In black mourn I, all fears scorn I,
Love hath forlorn me, living in thrall:
Heart is bleeding, all help needing—
O cruel speeding!—freighted with gall!
My shepherd's pipe can sound no deal,
My wether's bell rings doleful knell;
My curtal dog, that wont to have played,
Plays not at all, but seems afraid;
With sighs so deep, procure to weep,
In howling wise, to see my doleful plight.
How sighs resound through heartless ground,
Like a thousand vanquished men in bloody fight!

Clear wells spring not, sweet birds sing not,
Green plants bring not forth their dye:
Herds stand weeping, flocks all sleeping,
Nymphs back peeping fearfully:
All our pleasure known to us poor swains,
All our merry meetings on the plains,
All our evening sport from us is fled,
All our love is lost, for love is dead.

Farewell, sweet lass, thy like ne'er was
For a sweet content, the cause of all my moan:
Poor Corydon must live alone,
Other help for him I see that there is none.

18

Whenas thine eye hath chose the dame,
And stalled the deer that thou shouldst strike,
Let reason rule things worthy blame,
As well as fancy partial might:
    Take counsel of some wiser head,
    Neither too young, nor yet unwed

And when thou com'st thy tale to tell,
Smooth not thy tongue with filèd talk,
Lest she some subtle practice smell—
A cripple soon can find a halt—
    But plainly say thou lov'st her well,
    And set thy person forth to sell

And to her will frame all thy ways;
Spare not to spend—and chiefly there
Where thy desert may merit praise,
By ringing in thy lady's ear:
    The strongest castle, tower, and town,
    The golden bullet beats it down.

Serve always with assurèd trust,
And in thy suit be humble-true;
Unless thy lady prove unjust,
Seek never thou to choose anew:
    When time shall serve, be thou not slack
    To proffer, though she put thee back.

What though her frowning brows be bent,
Her cloudy looks will clear ere night;
And then too late she will repent
That thus dissembled her delight;
 And twice desire, ere it be day,
 That which with scorn she put away.

What though she strive to try her strength,
And ban and brawl, and say thee nay,
Her feeble force will yield at length,
When craft hath taught her thus to say—
 "Had women been so strong as men,
 In faith you had not had it then."

The wiles and guiles that women work,
Dissembled with an outward show,
The tricks and toys that in them lurk,
The cock that treads them shall not know.
 Have you not heard it said full oft,
 A woman's nay doth stand for naught?

Think women love to strive with men,
To sin and never for to saint:
There is no heaven; be holy then
When time with age shall them attaint.
 Were kisses all the joys in bed,
 One woman would another wed.

But soft! enough—too much I fear;
For if my mistress hear my song;
She will not stick to round me on th'ear,
To teach my tongue to be so long;
 Yet will she blush, here be it said,
 To hear her secrets so bewrayed.

The Phoenix
and Turtle

THE PHOENIX AND TURTLE

Let the bird of loudest lay,
On the sole Arabian tree,
Herald sad and trumpet be,
To whose sound chaste wings obey.

But thou shrieking harbinger,
Foul precurrer of the fiend,
Augur of the fever's end,
To this troop come thou not near!

From this session interdict
Every fowl of tyrant wing,
Save the eagle, feathered king:
Keep the obsequy so strict.

Let the priest in surplice white,
That defunctive music can,
Be the death-divining swan,
Lest the requiem lack his right.

And thou, treble-dated crow,
That thy sable gender mak'st
With the breath thou giv'st and tak'st
'Mongst our mourners shalt thou go.

Here the anthem doth commence—
Love and constancy is dead;
Phoenix and the turtle fled
In a mutual flame from hence.

So they loved, as love in twain
Had the essence but in one;
Two distincts, division none:
Number there in love was slain.

Hearts remote, yet not asunder;
Distance, and no space was seen
'Twixt the turtle and his queen:
But in them it were a wonder.

So between them love did shine,
That the turtle saw his right
Flaming in the phoenix' sight;
Either was the other's mine.

Property was thus appalled,
That the self was not the same
Single nature's double name
Neither two nor one was called.

Reason, in itself confounded,
Saw division grow together;
To themselves yet either neither,
Simple were so well compounded;

That it cried, "How true a twain
Seemeth this concordant one!
Love hath reason, reason none,
If what parts can so remain."

Whereupon it made this threne
To the phoenix and the dove,
Co-supremes and stars of love,
As chorus to their tragic scene.

THRENOS

Beauty, truth, and rarity,
Grace in all simplicity,
Here enclosed in cinders lie.

Death is now the phoenix' nest;
And the turtle's loyal breast
To eternity doth rest,

Leaving no posterity—
'Twas not their infirmity,
It was married chastity.

Truth may seem, but cannot be;
Beauty, brag, but 'tis not she;
Truth and beauty buried be.

To this urn let those repair
That are either true or fair;
For these dead birds sigh a prayer.

INDEX OF FIRST LINES OF THE SONNETS

(Note: numbers refer to the sonnet's position in the sequence)

No more be grieved at that which thou hast done: 35
No, Time, thou shalt not boast that I do change!   123
Not from the stars do I my judgment pluck   14
Not marble nor the gilded monuments   55
Not mine own fears, nor the prophetic soul   107
O, call not me to justify the wrong   139
O, for my sake do you with Fortune chide   111
O, from what power hast thou this powerful might   150
O, how I faint when I of you do write   80
O, how much more doth beauty beauteous seem   54
O, how thy worth with manners may I sing   39
O, lest the world should task you to recite   72
O me, what eyes hath Love put in my head   148
O, never say that I was false of heart   109
O, that you were yourself! But, love, you are   13
O thou, my lovely boy, who in thy power   126
O, truant Muse, what shall be thy amends   101
Or I shall live your epitaph to make   81
Or whether doth my mind, being crowned with you   114
Poor soul, the center of my sinful earth   146
Say that thou didst forsake me for some fault   89
Shall I compare thee to a summer's day?   18
Sin of self-love possesseth all mine eye   62
Since brass, nor stone, nor earth, nor boundless sea 65
Since I left you, mine eye is in my mind   113
So am I as the rich, whose blessèd key   52
So are you to my thoughts as food to life   75
So is it not with me as with that Muse   21
So, now I have confessed that he is thine   134
So oft have I invoked thee for my Muse   78
So shall I live, supposing thou art true   93
Some glory in their birth, some in their skill   91
Some say, thy fault is youth, some, wantonness   96
Sweet love, renew thy force; be it not said   56
Take all my loves, my love, yea, take them all   40